RECONSTRUCTION

The Battle for Democracy

RECONSTRUCTION

The Battle for Democracy

1865-1876

BY JAMES S. ALLEN

Author of The Negro Question in the U. S.

INTERNATIONAL PUBLISHERS, NEW YORK

CONTENTS

ILLUSTRATIONS

EDITOR'S FOREWORD

UNTIL recently, the history of Reconstruction has been left to the not very tender mercies of the Bourbon and the Philistine. The result has been a completely distorted picture of one of the most significant epochs in American history. For the most part our historians have hidden the revolutionary content of Reconstruction behind a veil of vituperation, have entirely misrepresented the rôle of the Negro people and have shamefully besmirched the heroic leadership of Stevens and his Radical associates. One looks in vain to find in the writings of most American historians a recognition of the revolutionary character of the period following the Civil War. The consolidation of power by the industrial bourgeoisie, the establishment of a bourgeois-democratic dictatorship, the democratic and agrarian upsurge in the South, the forging of such revolutionary weapons as the Union League clubs and citizen militia units—all of these have been either ignored or at best glossed over.

Similarly, the part played by the Negro people in the Reconstruction of the South has been disregarded or treated with contempt. Our historians have gone out of their way to demonstrate the ignorance and stupidity of "banjo-twanging, melody-singing" Negroes, the gullible prey of "carpetbaggers" and "scalawags." They have been apparently oblivious of the

7

battle which the freedmen fought for democracy, land and civil rights in the South, of their active participation in the struggles of the period not as the mute followers of the bourgeoisie but as their independent allies.

The revolutionary leadership of the Radical Republicans has likewise been misrepresented by many historians and biographers, more so recently than ever before. Thaddeus Stevens and Charles Sumner—leading representatives of the Parliamentary Left—have become the emissaries of the devil, "apostles of propaganda and hate." In his *Age of Hate, Andrew Johnson and the Radicals* (1930), George F. Milton pictures Stevens as a drunkard and an "inveterate gambler," and Sumner as an "eerie, evil genius...spinning tenuous spider-webs of...Negro equality." At the same time, Milton attempts to rehabilitate the traitor of the revolution, the man whom Wendell Phillips once aptly dubbed "Jefferson Davis Johnson."

Milton is the contemporary prototype of John W. Burgess, leading exponent of the Bourbon school. This ex-Confederate soldier consciously endeavored at the turn of the century to rewrite the history of Reconstruction from a Southern viewpoint. In his *Reconstruction and the Constitution* (1902), Burgess characterizes the period as the rule of "the uncivilized Negroes over the whites...." To him, the North must admit the failure of Reconstruction if "a real national brotherhood" was ever to be achieved. The main lines laid down by Burgess have found their most nauseating expression in *The Tragic Era* (1929) of Claude Bowers. Correctly described by Dr. Du Bois as "a classic example of historical propaganda of the cheapest sort," this work bewails the misfortunes of the Southern people who were "literally put to the torture." The Negro is naturally excluded from the above category. Bowers attempts to vindicate not only Andrew Johnson, but also the "brilliant" spokesmen of the old slave South. The latter are given "their proper place in the dramatic struggle for the preservation of Southern civilization...."

Besides the Bourbon, the Philistine has contributed his share to the distortion of the historiography of Reconstruction. In his *History of the United States* (1906), James F. Rhodes, for some time considered the leading historian of the period,[*] explicitly condemns the Northern policy of Reconstruction as "repressive, uncivilized and unsuccessful" and, as an enthusiastic exponent of "conciliation," hails the withdrawal of Federal troops from the South as essential to the overthrow of "carpet-bag-negro governments by the educated and property-holding people of the several States." Thoroughly convinced of Negro inferiority, Rhodes feels it a shame that "the most degraded Negro could vote, while Robert E. Lee, Wade Hampton [and] Alexander Stephens ... could not."

The same anti-Negro bias is to be found in the work of the late Professor William A. Dunning of Columbia University. In his *Reconstruction, Political and Economic* (1907) he sees "intelligence and political capacity" on one side, and "no pride of race and no aspiration or ideal" on the other. To Dunning, the plight of decent white men trying to maintain "their rights and their property against the flood of barbarism" is most pathetic. A group of graduate students, many of whom came from the South, gathered around Dunning. State monographs appeared at Columbia and other universities. Though these treatises are, for the most part, violently anti-Negro, they nevertheless contain much valuable material for the purposes of re-

[*] For a critique of Rhodes and his methods, see J. R. Lynch, *Some Historical Errors of James F. Rhodes* (Boston, 1922).

interpretation. Francis B. Simkins' and Robert H. Woody's *South Carolina During Reconstruction* (1932), though at times confused, is especially worthy of mention.

Although the Bourbon and the Philistine ignore the revolutionary implications of Reconstruction, the liberal bourgeois historian does not. In his *Rise of American Civilization* (1927), Charles A. Beard, leading exponent of the school, recognizes that the revolution, released during the Civil War, continued during Reconstruction. The period completed the ruin of the former slave obligarchy and the triumph of the industrial bourgeoisie. How the latter consolidated its position is shown in detail by Howard K. Beale in his *Critical Year, A Study of Andrew Johnson and Reconstruction* (1930). Yet, despite a promising beginning, liberal writers see only one side of the revolutionary picture. Failing to appreciate fully the class dynamics of historical development, they do not distinguish clearly between the various class forces at work. This leads them to ignore some of the most important revolutionary phenomena of Reconstruction. Not least is the part played by the freedmen during the period. They accept uncritically the traditional rôle of the Negro people in the Reconstruction of the South. To Beard, "... the freedmen were in no way prepared to become an effective factor in the new order of society ... they were powerless in the hands of the governing group that directed the revolution and reconstruction from Washington...." Beale practically takes a similar view of the situation, a view strengthened by his belief that the Negro plantation hands were not only illiterate but "had no conception of ... the meaning of terms like government, morality, suffrage, or even free labor."

A refreshing antidote to the traditional acceptance of Negro inferiority and passiveness is offered by Du

Bois in his praiseworthy *Black Reconstruction* (1935). This is a spirited defense of the Negro in Reconstruction and of the Radical policies of the period. Du Bois portrays the fight of the freedmen for democracy, their work in establishing the first public school system in the South for blacks and whites, and their heroic struggle against the counter-revolution. Du Bois' failure to grasp the fundamental bourgeois character of the revolution leads him to the mistaken notion that what was occurring in the South during Reconstruction "was one of the most extraordinary experiments in Marxism that the world, before the Russian Revolution, had seen." Du Bois therefore very naturally falls into the error of characterizing the Reconstruction governments of the epoch as dictatorships of labor (that is, the proletariat) despite the fact that at the time such a type of dictatorship was out of the question. What was actually established in the South during these years was a bourgeois-democratic dictatorship varying according to specific state conditions and existing for varied lengths of time.

This point is clearly advanced in the present volume, which comes as an invigorating counteraction to the Bourbon and bourgeois distortions of the period. In Marxist fashion, the author first of all analyzes Reconstruction as the second phase of the revolution inaugurated by the Civil War and shows how (broadly speaking) the period accomplished its purpose of preventing the return of chattel slavery and of consolidating the power of the industrial bourgeoisie. Secondly, he carefully deals with the class dynamics of the era and clearly distinguishes the various class forces at play. He presents the rôle of the farmers, workers and freedmen and discusses their relationship to the dominant social phenomena of Reconstruction: the rise of the industrial capitalists and the submergence of the old slave oligarchy.

In the third place, the present volume deals with the democratic character of the revolution and with the attempt to establish democracy in the South. The extension of civil and political rights, the participation of Negroes in state and county governments, the convocation of people's assemblies, the establishment of a public system of education for both races—all are graphically described. Similarly the forging of revolutionary weapons, such as popular government (the much maligned "carpetbag" régimes), Union League clubs and volunteer defense corps, is presented. The work of the Negro people in these revolutionary bodies as well as their conscious struggle for democracy and civil rights are also set forth. Thus, the true relationship of the Negro masses to Reconstruction clearly emerges and the freedman is shown to be the independent ally of the bourgeoisie restricted in his activities by the limits of the period and of the revolution.

Lastly, the struggle between revolution and counter-revolution is described and reasons assigned for the triumph of the latter. The author attributes the defeat of Radical Reconstruction to the vacillations of the bourgeois revolution and to the regrouping of class forces in the nation. The Northern bourgeoisie, by hesitating to confiscate the plantations of the old slavocracy and divide them up among the freedmen, permitted the emergence in the South of a semi-feudal agrarian economy based on share-cropping. This, in turn, made more difficult coöperation between Southern small white landowners and Negro share-tenants. It likewise allowed the large planters to retain their estates, thus making it easier for them to regain political power. Similarly, amnesty to ex-Confederate leaders, toleration of the reactionary press and half-hearted measures against counter-revolutionary bands (K.K.K. and others) played into the hands of the former slave oligarchy.

The re-alignment of class forces also made possible the victory of reaction. The rise of large-scale industry shifted the attack from the old to the new oligarchy. Farmers and workers revolted attempting to strip the "bloated plutocracy of its ill-gotten gains." While this was occurring, the labor movement was reaching a high level of development in regard to national organization and independent political action. This promising beginning, however, did not prevent sections of organized labor, together with the farmers, from tending to associate themselves with the Bourbon element through the Democratic Party, instead of forming a broad progressive coalition which would include the Negro and safeguard the victories won by the revolution. The rising tide of discontent caused the industrial bourgeoisie to sacrifice the Negro in order to better defend itself. In the meantime, the reactionary Southern planting classes, realizing the plight of the freedmen, seized the opportunity offered. They split the temporary alliance between the upland white farmers of the South and the Negro masses, unleashed a White Terror, established a number of *coup d'état* governments and in 1877 came to an understanding with the industrial bourgeoisie. Counter-revolution in the South was accompanied by bourgeois reaction in the North; the suppression of the great railroad strike of 1877 stands as a bloody testimonial to the "new dispensation."

The democratic heritage of Reconstruction and the unfinished tasks of the revolution are clearly set forth in this book. From 1865 to 1876, an attempt was made to establish democracy in the South; the freedmen secured the right to vote, enjoyed civil liberties and participated in the affairs of state. During this crucial period, the Negro was aided in his struggle by the then progressive Republican Party. The latter, however, soon shamefully deserted its ally and literally left him to the mercies of the reactionary forces. Even though democracy was destroyed in the South as a result of this perfidy, the heroic fight of the Negroes and their allies during Reconstruction still remains as one of the most brilliant chapters in American history. Today, with the help of the working class and other progressive elements, the Negro people can complete the unfinished tasks of revolutionary Reconstruction and thereby secure for themselves suffrage, civil rights and land.

The present volume is designed to introduce clearly, within the limitations of a small book, the principal revolutionary aspects of the Reconstruction period. This work does not presume to be definitive. Neither has an attempt been made to write a comprehensive history of the epoch. Consequently, the specialist and student in the field will find certain phenomena not germane to the principal tendencies discussed, ignored or only touched upon in passing. The author has devoted most of his attention to the South, but even here chiefly to those states in which the Radical Reconstruction policies were most completely applied and in which the revolution reached its highest expression. It is hoped that the present book will encourage further Marxist investigation into one of the most significant epochs in the revolutionary and democratic traditions of the American people.

Richard Enmale

RECONSTRUCTION

The Battle for Democracy

*"De bottom rail's on de top,
An' we's gwine to keep it dar."*

TO ISABELLE

FIRST PHASE OF THE REVOLUTION

Clash of Social Systems

IN the American Republic, the revolution against England created that political shell within which a second revolution matured. A society based upon free farming and free labor emerged in the North, while the South developed a society based upon chattel slavery. Each produced its distinctive social and political institutions, within the framework of a single Constitution and a single Republic. Social development in the North proceeded along capitalist and democratic lines. In the South, the slave oligarchy established itself as a barrier to the free development of capitalism and as the very antithesis of democracy. War between the two antagonistic systems was inevitable.

The slavocracy tolerated the central republican government only as long as it could be controlled and used as a weapon for the protection and the extension of the slave power. With deft hands, the plantation barons were able to parry the capitalist power in the North by allying with themselves the commercial and banking interests engaged in the cotton trade and bound in other ways with the slave economy. As Karl Marx put it: "The Union became the slave of the 300,000 slaveholders who rule the South."

During the decade preceding the election of Lincoln, the slaveowners demonstrated how it was possible to use the Republic to block the aspirations of that class for which historical development had evolved demo-

17

cratic forms of government. In 1856, both houses of Congress were controlled by the Democrats, the President and his cabinet were in full sympathy with the leaders of the slavocracy, seven of the nine Justices of the Supreme Court were either owners of plantations or sympathetic to slavery. According to Seward, all the principal committees in the Senate were dominated by the slaveholders and only too willing to initiate legislation in the interests of the slavocracy.

Harbingers of the gathering storm were the battle between the pioneer farmers and the slaveholders for the possession of Kansas and the birth of the Republican Party. The central point of the program on which Lincoln was elected was the restriction of slavery to its then existing boundaries. The slave aristocracy recognized the first, although feeble, expression of the revolutionary upheaval. No longer able to turn the Republic to its own purposes, the slave power discarded it and set out to subdue the gathering revolution. Secession, the fatal shot at Fort Sumter, the Confederate call to arms followed in rapid succession as the slavocracy initiated the counter-revolution.

The sectional nature of the conflict and the geographic division of the contending classes have obscured the essential revolutionary nature of the Civil War. But this conflict was basically a revolution of a bourgeois democratic character, in which the bourgeoisie was fighting for power against the landed aristocracy. The revolution assumed the features of a long-drawn-out war, in which the contending classes commanded formally organized armies and sought to win by conquering the other's territory. This peculiarity in the form of the revolution arose from the fact that two opposing systems had developed in separate areas of the Republic. But the conflict was as fundamental a social revolution as it would have been if the slave system were uniformly spread throughout the country and the middle class, evolved in the course of commercial and capitalist development, had risen to take power.

Lincoln and Stevens: Two Courses in the Revolution

HISTORY was not ambiguous in the task allotted to the bourgeoisie. The further expansion of capitalism required the annihilation of the slave power which at every turn placed obstacles in the path of northern industry and free agriculture, and acted like a drag on the young and progressive bourgeoisie. Capitalist industry had to be assured, above all, of its own home market. This was the prime economic force which propelled the North in its struggle against the South. The bourgeoisie needed to dominate the whole country, to achieve national unity under its own wing, to explore, broaden, round out and conquer the market at home. This is the driving force of capitalism in progress, in the period of its expansion and growth. It was expressed in the battlecry of "Save the Union!" with which the North took the field.

But to achieve this, the bourgeoisie had to go beyond the mere defeat of the slave power in war. The minimum requirements of the epoch included also the complete destruction of the economic and political power of the landed barons. This power rested upon slavery. Emancipation and bourgeois freedom for the Negro would strike the death blow to the pre-capitalist power of the South.

Compromises and vacillations crippled the bourgeoisie from the start of the war. It had been forced to embark on the course of revolution by the offensive of counter-revolution. On the eve of the conflict the representatives of the free North in Congress haggled over constitutional forms, conceding one victory after another to the slave power. The slaveowners, allied with the Copperhead Democrats (representing for the most part the commercial and banking interests of the North) pressed from one advantage to another, easily finding legal garments in the wardrobe of the Constitution with which to clothe their usurpations. Torn between the gathering forces of the industrial bourgeoisie and the insistent, self-reliant slave power, Northern statesmen continued right up to the war to cede one point after another to their opponent.

With secession declared, with the Confederacy in being, with the "irrepressible conflict" already inaugurated, the Northerners continued to bury their noses in law books, seeking further compromises for their revolution. Ready for any compromise short of disunion, Lincoln entered the battlefield with the cry of "Save the Union!" when the supreme demand of the moment was the full-throated challenge, "Emancipation!"

Even through the first two years of the war, bourgeois democracy hesitated to adopt revolutionary methods. The President and Congress were preoccupied with the "constitutionality" of financing the war, of raising an army, of even the war itself, when everything depended upon a quick, decisive offensive.

Thaddeus Stevens, the clear-sighted revolutionist, could proclaim in Congress: "Constitution now is silent and only the Laws of War obtain." But the middle classes could not lead a consistent revolutionary battle. Lincoln, their greatest spokesman, advanced only with hesitation and with great wavering. This led Marx to remark in a letter to Engels, chiding him for his lack of faith in the final victory of the North caused by its vacillating policies and its early defeats:

In my opinion all this will take another turn. In the end the North will make war seriously, adopt revolutionary methods and throw over the domination of the border slaves statesmen. A single Negro regiment would have a remarkable effect on Southern nerves....

The long and short of the business seems to me to be that a war of this kind must be conducted on revolutionary lines, while the Yankees have so far been trying to conduct it constitutionally.[1]

Eventually the North used revolutionary means to carry on a revolution. But in the meantime, two courses in the revolution were making themselves felt and the battle between the two wings of the bourgeois democracy was becoming sharp. Lincoln shied away from the full historical tasks of the epoch. An immediate Declaration of Emancipation at the outbreak of the war, even if it amounted at first to nothing but a declaration of policy, would have released much sooner a tremendous revolutionary force to play havoc with the slaveowners' flank. Only after Union victories in the West and in Kentucky and Tennessee, when it became apparent that nothing was to be gained by negotiations with the border states' slaveowners, did Lincoln issue the Emancipation Proclamation—almost two years after the outbreak of war.

The same hesitancy to apply revolutionary, "unconstitutional" methods hindered the Lincoln wing from arming the Negroes sooner and thus winning a powerful ally early in the struggle. In time, under pressure from the Negroes themselves and from the revolutionary bourgeoisie, Lincoln finally gave in on this point, too.

The vacillating Center, led by Lincoln, did finally adopt some of the inevitable revolutionary weapons. However, the course of the Lincoln wing of the revolution was the course of compromise, of hesitancy when compromise would no longer do, of wavering before the onslaught of the landed aristocracy, of willingness to retreat and withdraw from the struggle at the earliest opportunity.

On the other hand, the bourgeois revolution also produced its more direct agents, who, while not always conscious of their rôle, held the prod of progress in their hands and goaded those who wavered, uncertain and afraid before the immensity of the task confronting them. Such a revolutionist, above every one else, was Thaddeus Stevens, who gathered around himself the best representatives of the industrial bourgeoisie and the Abolitionist democracy.

The differences between the two wings of the bourgeoisie did not lead to decisive struggle until after the war, but clear divergence in policy and tactics was evident from the beginning of the conflict. Stevens in the House and Charles Sumner in the Senate, and a growing number of followers, pooh-poohed the Lincolnian awe of the Constitution. When Lincoln rebuked General Frémont for liberating captured slaves, Stevens declared, "we have put a sword into one hand of our generals and shackles into the other. Free men are not inspired by such mingled music." At the beginning of 1862, Stevens demanded universal freedom and, referring to the slaves who worked the plantations while their masters went off to war, declared: "Those who now furnish the means of war, but who are the natural enemies of slaveholders, must be made our allies." He was just as persistent in demanding that the Negroes be armed and suggested in a speech in Congress, in July 1862, "sending the army throughout the whole slave population of the South, asking them to go from their masters, take the weapons which we furnish and join us in this war of freedom against traitors and rebels. Until that policy is adopted, I have no hope of success."

There were those who, while claiming to side with

the Union, expressed fear that slave insurrections would follow upon any proclamation of emancipation. "What puerile inconsistency!" stormed Stevens. "Which is more to be abhorred—a rebellion of slaves challenging their masters, or a rebellion of free men fighting to murder the Nation? You send forth your sons and brothers to shoot and saber and bayonet the insurgents, but you hesitate to break the bonds of their slaves to reach the same end." [2]

Stevens fought against compromise and demanded that revolutionary means be employed to conquer the slaveowners and destroy their system. The bourgeois revolution found its true leader in Stevens, although it was reluctant to accept him, frightened by the passion, the stubbornness, the fighting partisan spirit (as if revolution can mean anything but partisanship!), the logical expression of the policy demanded by the revolutionary epoch. The distinct contribution of the Abolitionists had been that they recognized the necessity and inevitability of emancipation. It was Stevens, however, more than any one else among the bourgeois leaders, who realized the whole revolutionary content of the period, and who led the forces which eventually seized the reins of the revolution from the hands of the petty-bourgeois vacillators.

Stake of the Working Class in the Revolution

THE bourgeoisie could not enter on the course of revolution without at the same time drawing along with it the masses in both the North and the South, thus broadening the scope of the social upheaval. The movement against the slave power found its mass support among the workers of the North and, to a lesser degree, sections of the free workers of the South, among the farmers of the North and many parts of the South and, with rapidly increasing significance, among the Negroes. But this was not an undifferentiated mass gathered on the side of the bourgeoisie. There were conflicting interests among the bourgeois strata which came to the surface continually: the conflict between the rising industrial bourgeoisie and the commercial and banking middle class; between the industrial bourgeoisie and the farmers; between the landlords and the landless farmers.

But the most fundamental antagonism among the forces on the side of the North was between the bourgeoisie and the proletariat. This was a bourgeois revolution and even its most advanced spokesmen, such as Stevens and Sumner, did not go beyond the bounds of bourgeois democracy. In the Abolition movement a cleavage had arisen between the bourgeois and the working-class Abolitionists, the latter demanding not only an end to chattel slavery but to wage slavery as well. A recurrent refrain in working-class agitation during that period was the slogan: "Down with all slavery, both chattel and wages." In the North the rise of capitalism was accompanied by the inevitable struggle between employers and workers.

At the beginning of the war the organized labor movement was extremely weak, having been unable to recover from the onslaught of the crisis of 1857. It was also affected by the general collapse of industry which reflected the state of apoplexy of the bourgeoisie when faced with the actual conflict. The working class, despite the relatively late period in the development of capitalism in which the revolution occurred, was still too small, not yet located strategically enough in capitalist economy, and too immature politically to have left the imprint of its own class position clearly and unequivocally on the course of events. In general, it followed in the wake of the bourgeoisie and supported it in the struggle against the slave power, without at the same time entering the struggle as a class on its own account, or with as much consciousness of its own aims as had been the case in the bourgeois revolutions in Europe in the nineteenth century.

The more advanced sections of the labor movement entered the conflict with a clear realization that the class aims of the workers were for the moment bound up with the fulfillment of the bourgeois revolution. Many Socialist leaders and German emigrés of the 1848 revolution, among them Joseph Weydemeyer, who was a close friend of Karl Marx, served as officers in the Union Army. William Sylvis, organizer of the Molders' Union and the outstanding labor leader of the period, helped to recruit a company from among the members of his union and for a time served as a volunteer in the Northern Army. "Many of the wisest of the labor men," wrote McNeill, a contemporary trade unionist, were "of the opinion that no great progress could be made until after the destruction of the chattel slave system." [3]

Among certain backward and unorganized sections of the workers (principally in such banking and trading centers as New York and Boston where the influence of the slavocracy and its Copperhead allies was strong) the war was not received with great enthusiasm, and was even violently opposed. On the other hand, if one recalls the vacillations of the bourgeoisie in the face of its own revolution, its stammering utterance of only a half revolutionary slogan ("Save the Union!")—then the ready response of the organized workers appears in its full historic significance. This is especially striking when it is remembered that these workers were keenly aware of what seemed to them the more immediate struggle against wage slavery and were not generally aware of the priority of the struggle against chattel slavery. At the first call for men whole unions enlisted in a body. Both the subordination of the working class to the needs of the bourgeois revolution and the decisiveness with which it rose to the historic task are expressed in this cryptic sentence in the minutes of a Philadelphia trade union: "It having been resolved to enlist with Uncle Sam for the war, this union stands adjourned until either the Union is safe or we are whipped." [4]

The bourgeois revolution itself gave birth to revolutionary energy among the masses in proportion to the decisiveness of the struggle and the consciousness of its aims. Men like Stevens and other bourgeois revolutionists paid a direct service to the working class in that they educated the masses in the tasks of the bourgeois revolution, drew wider sections into conscious political activity and thus helped to release energies later to be utilized in battles between the erstwhile allies.

The working class had a direct stake in the bourgeois revolution. The slave power blocked the path of the further development of the labor movement. Slavery had to be abolished before the solution of the question of wage-slavery could be undertaken with any degree of success in America. The destruction of the slave power was the basis for real national unity and the further development of capitalism, which would produce conditions most favorable for the growth of the labor movement. The American working class could then be in a position to enter upon the scene of history in its own capacity as a revolutionary class. The relation of the proletariat to the bourgeois revolution under nineteenth-century conditions was concisely summarized by Engels in his discussion of the European revolutions of 1848-51.

The working class movement itself never is independent, never is of an exclusively proletarian character—he wrote—until all the different factions of the middle class, and particularly its most progressive faction, the large manufacturers, have conquered political power, and remodeled the state according to their wants. It is then that the inevitable conflict between the employer and the employed becomes imminent, and cannot be adjourned any longer; that the working class can no longer be put off with delusive hopes and promises never to be realized; that the great problem of the nineteenth century, the abolition of the proletariat, is at last brought forward fairly and in its proper light.[5]

Although the bourgeois revolution developed in the United States under different conditions than in Europe, the fundamental class relationships were similar. The middle class was engaged in a revolutionary struggle against a landed aristocracy. Large-scale manufacturing was only beginning to emerge, spurred to rapid growth by the Civil War itself. The middle class had seized the reins of government and, in the course of the struggle against counter-revolution, would be forced to relinquish them to the industrial bourgeoisie. The petty-bourgeoisie in town and country wavered, sections of it remaining sympathetic to the slavocracy. For the middle class stood between the two principal contending classes, the rising industrial bourgeoisie, which promised a new oligarchy, and the slavocracy whose oligarchy they had already endured. And new, disquieting revolutionary forces were arising: the proletariat in the North which was already springing into action at the close of the war; and the new body of freedmen, of landless peasants in the South, the mainstay of the bourgeois revolution during the decade after the war.

The stage was being cleared of outworn and hackneyed properties to make way for a new and contemporary drama in which the chief protagonists would be the bourgeoisie and the proletariat. Consoling himself on his keen disappointment with the wavering of the North and its policy of compromise, Engels, early in the war, drew a very pertinent moral. "On the one hand," he wrote Marx, "it is well that the bourgeois republic has so thoroughly disgraced itself in America also, so that in the future it can never again be preached on its own merits, but only as a means and transitional form to the social revolution, although one is peeved that a lousy oligarchy of only half the number of inhabitants has proved itself just as strong as the clumsy, big, helpless democracy." [6] The bourgeois republic "as a means and a transition form to the social revolution"—this was the main historical import of the bourgeois revolution to the proletariat.

"The Paroquet of the Wh-e Ho-e," a caricature of President Johnson.—*Harpers Weekly*, March 21, 1868.

CHAPTER I

THE JOHNSON REACTION

The New Phase of Revolution

WITH the defeat of the South on the battlefield and the emancipation of the slaves the revolution had completed only its first cycle. The slaveowners had been conquered and the institution of chattel slavery had been abolished. A new phase, involving the complete transformation of southern society, now opened.

The former ruling class had been defeated: would it also be deposed? Chattel slavery had been abolished: would the landed estates remain? The slave institutions and the slave oligarchy had been destroyed: would bourgeois democracy take their place?

These quickly emerged as the issues of the new phase of the revolution. If the bourgeoisie was to maintain national dominance, it could not permit the landed aristocracy to regain power in the South. All grounds for counter-revolution and restoration had to be removed. For, once the former slaveholders regained power in the South, they could win, with the aid of allies in the North, dominance in the national government.

But what class was to replace the former ruling class in the South? A well-developed middle class, such as existed in the North, was not present in the South. In the towns and cities there was a small commercial middle class which had subsisted principally in the capacity of middleman for the slaveowner. The really

big plantation business had been carried on through
the cotton factors of New York and New Orleans or
directly with firms in England. The urban middle class,
as a matter of fact, only began to emerge on any important scale as a result of the changes brought about
by the Civil War.

Far more important were the small landed proprietors and tenants, the whites of the non-plantation up-
country, who had suffered under the slave oligarchy.
Many of these sections had been pro-Union during the
war. "Poor whites" drafted into the Confederate Army
had deserted in large numbers. These peasant proprietors and tenants, hungry for more land and for democratic rights, could provide a part of the popular base
for democracy in the South.

There was no proletariat to speak of, for the same
reason that no industrial bourgeoisie existed in the
South. A few factories were scattered here and there.
Most of the workers were artisans, either in the towns
and cities or on the plantations. There had been more
slave skilled-workers than free. But a proletariat had
as yet hardly formed itself, much less appeared as a
class able to exert an independent force in the transformation of the South.

Destined to play a pivotal rôle in the revolution
were the newly emancipated Negro masses, overwhelmingly predominant in the population of the plantation
area, the very stronghold of landed power. If this was
to be a people's revolution, they would have to be the
core of it; if democracy was to be established they
would have to be its chief bearers.

The former slaves could be drawn into the revolution as an active ally of the bourgeoisie only if their
demands were incorporated in the general program of
the bourgeoisie. These demands did not halt at emancipation from chattel slavery. Emancipation was merely

the springboard from which the revolution in the South could leap far ahead. Once the former slaves were set into motion, the revolution had to assume an agrarian and democratic character.

This was the logic of the situation. The bourgeoisie could not avoid it, although it came to adopt revolutionary methods only after a fatal delay. The issues were clearly projected: confiscation of the landed estates for the benefit of the landless, disfranchisement of the land barons and Negro suffrage. These were the chief economic and political steps demanded by the revolution. Anything short of the fulfillment of these minimum requirements would eventually lead to the victory of reaction.

Spontaneous events in the South even before the end of the war were raising sharply the issues at stake and pronouncing a revolutionary course for their solution. The recruiting of Negroes into the Union Army and the arming of slaves were the first revolutionary steps. In the words of Frederick Douglass, the nation had unchained "against her foes her powerful black hand." Almost 200,000 Negroes were under arms by the end of the war. Free Negroes of the North and South, ex-slaves in the territory occupied by the Northern Army, and slaves fleeing from plantations in the interior had rushed to arms.

The arming of the Negroes introduced a new and vital force. The numerous slave revolts had been defeated in their isolation; but this was slave insurrection on a tremendous scale. Thousands of Denmark Veseys, Nat Turners, Shields, Greens, Browns and Copelands were in motion together with a powerful ally, in the stream of revolution. The ex-slaves, the "ignorant, illiterate mass," imparted a revolutionary frenzy to the army—"a terrible 'army with banners,'" encouraging the Negroes to engage in pillage, fraterniz-

ing with them, and telling them that they were free."
Charleston, the scene of Vesey's defeat, became the
scene of his victory. The first troops entering the city
were headed by a Negro soldier bearing a banner inscribed with the word "Liberty." The Negro regiments,
led by the famous Fifty-fourth of Massachusetts, followed singing "John Brown's Body." The streets rang
with the cheers of the ex-slaves. Negro troops searched
every house in the city to proclaim freedom and seize
firearms and abandoned property. Slave pens and the
auction blocks were destroyed and burned.[1]

Scenes such as these were repeated in every new
town or city occupied by the Union Army. The newly-
won liberty knew no bounds. The rough, calloused
hand of the ex-slave brushed aside the polished lumber
of the aristocracy. "Their whole manner has changed,"
wailed a maternal plantation owner. "They took to
calling their former owners by their last name without
any title before it...dropped the pleasant term of
mistress...walked about with guns upon their shoulders."[2] Landless peasants, yesterday slaves, with guns
upon their shoulders—foreboding, menacing.

The first impulse was to destroy the outward implements of slave exploitation. When Port Royal, S. C.,
fell to the Union Army in November 1861, the freedmen occupied houses, tore down churches and used the
lumber to build cabins for themselves. They broke
open church organs and blew the pipes in the streets.
Churches for cabins and church organ pipes for blow-
ing in freedom—the revolution in its first stages of
ecstasy.

The popular movement welled forth at the start.
The sun rose upon emancipation and set upon the
struggle for land and liberty.

The Parliamentary Struggle

IN proclaiming emancipation for the slaves and placing arms in their hands the bourgeoisie had precipitated the Negro masses into the very center of the revolution. Now they were pushing ahead, at first without the guidance of a clear program and without organization, towards the redistribution of the land and the attainment of political liberty. The slavocracy had realized full well the consistent course of revolution. The Confederate Congress, in its last address of March 1865, warned that the penalty for the defeat of the South in the war would be "the confiscation of the estates, which would be given to their former bondsmen." The land question, which we shall discuss in the next chapter, early became a pivot around which the revolution revolved.

The sweep of the revolution was converting the ex-slave into a fighter for bourgeois democracy. For him, bourgeois democracy meant first of all the possession of the land. The North had ordered the expropriation of the cotton of the slaveowners in conquered territory; but it stopped to draw its breath before the first, faltering expropriation of the land, the houses, the belongings of the landed aristocracy—and then faced right about. Under the first impulses of the revolution the ex-slaves advanced in a direct line towards the fulfillment of its tasks.

What would be the attitude of the bourgeoisie to this new force emerging upon the field of battle? Here was the mass base for a democratic transformation in the domain of the former slavocracy. It needed to be organized as an ally of the bourgeoisie to attain those ends in the South which were for the time common to both. Would the bourgeoisie seize upon this ally, help it organize and formulate a program, and channelize its energies towards the attainment of the aims of the revolution?

This was the key problem of strategy which confronted the bourgeoisie. This was the central problem of Reconstruction. The attempt to meet it divided Congress into hostile wings. The differences were so sharp that the parliamentary struggle was the most violent in American history, and a President was impeached and then acquitted by only one vote.

In its parliamentary form the real issue appeared in the question of the readmittance of the rebel states—or the "so-called states," as Stevens insisted—into the Union. The Right wing—the Johnson, parliamentary wing—would have restored the states easily and quickly with little change. The Left wing, led by Stevens, insisted upon a complete social reconstruction of the states before admittance. The Right would have called a halt to the revolution at the close of the war and made complete peace with the former slavocracy. The Left insisted upon the revolutionary consequences of the war.

In Congressional addresses, Presidential proclamations and campaign speeches, real issues were often buried by mountains of verbiage and tomes of constitutional law. The legal battle hinged around the status of the rebel states. Legislators, learned in constitutional law, but ignorant of the laws of revolution, argued the proposition back and forth: Are the states still in the Union or are they not? Lincoln, and later the Right, held that under the Constitution, the states could not secede and indeed had never seceded, eleven secession proclamations notwithstanding. Secession was the act not of the states but of disloyal persons in them. Therefore, those holy state entities, serenely impersonal and incapable of committing treason, were still in the Union, entitled to the full protection of the Constitution and the laws of the United States. Since it was not a question of admitting new states into the Union, but simply embracing a state which was temporarily erring (through no fault of its own, mind you!) the President should have the power of welcoming the prodigal after "it" had atoned to the President's satisfaction.

If the President had seen eye to eye with the Left on the central problem of Reconstruction, there would have been no argument to pick with this theoretical and abstract proposition. The real quarrel was not over the constitutional garb chosen to clothe Reconstruction, but over the course of Reconstruction itself.

At the end of 1863, Stevens was already arguing the simple proposition that the rebel states, having waged war and once vanquished, should be treated as conquered provinces. He did not press the point then, but when Reconstruction became the central problem at the end of the war, he gradually won the majority of Republicans for his point of view. According to this interpretation of the Constitution, the logical conclusion, as he expressed it later, followed: "The future condition of the conquered power depends on the will of the conqueror. They must come in as new states or remain as conquered provinces. Congress—the Senate and House of Representatives with the concurrence of the President—is the only power that can act in the matter." [3]

The leadership of the Left parliamentary wing of the revolution was in Congress; of the Right (after the death of Lincoln) in the executive chair. The parliamentary battle therefore assumed the form of a struggle between the President and Congress. It was hampered throughout by a religious, even fanatic, devotion to constitutional practice and displayed that peculiar devotion of the bourgeoisie to the letter, if not the spirit, of the law. Again, as during the Civil War, the bourgeoisie attempted to don revolution in a constitutional toga. The revolution tripped constantly in the folds of the ill-fitting garment.

Yet behind the verbiage of a law court, behind the controversy between the executive and legislative branches of government and between Federal and state rights, a fundamental class struggle was taking place. The rights of Congress, of President, of states were not the real issues. These were only the parliamentary expression, peculiar to American tradition and legality, of the real issues of the class struggle. Under the banner of state rights the former slavocracy attempted to restore itself and to prevent the intervention of the bourgeoisie. In the name of the rights of states, President Johnson and his faction of the middle class attempted to use the Presidency as a buffer against the industrial bourgeoisie. He was thrown into the arms of the former slavocracy and attempted to turn the executive post into the weapon of a revived Confederacy. The North returned from victorious war only to find a traitor in the most exalted post of the Union.

Lincoln's Plan of Reconstruction

IN the midst of the war, Lincoln, the Centrist, had already laid down a basis for the Right course in Reconstruction. The New Orleans area was occupied by Union forces in April 1862. The following August, Lincoln appointed the former mayor of New Orleans military governor of Louisiana and ordered an election for Congressional representatives for the State. These were seated in the House in February 1863, with very little objection.

Lincoln's plan was more comprehensively formulated in his Proclamation of Amnesty and Reconstruction on December 8, 1863. He extended full pardon, "with restoration of all rights of property, except as to slaves," to all those taking an oath of loyalty and allegiance to the United States and recognizing the abolition of slavery. All white Southerners were eligible for amnesty except members of the Confederate Government and high military officers in its army, members of the Federal Government or Union Army who had left posts to help the Confederates, and military officers who had treated Negroes in the Northern Army in any other manner than as prisoners of war.

On the basis of this oath Lincoln proposed to proceed with the restoration of the South. States would be readmitted into the Union as soon as loyal governments had been set up by one-tenth of the 1860 electorate, providing the voters had taken the oath of loyalty and the resulting state governments complied with the conditions of the oath. In addition, the loyal voters had to be qualified by the election law of these states in 1860. The new loyal governments thus organized could maintain, Lincoln pointed out, the constitution and general code of laws which were in force before the Civil War except for changes recognizing the abolition of slavery.

This plan represented a retreat even for Lincoln. At this time he had already declared the slaves free and authorized their recruitment into the Army. Yet the only positive steps he would take were to disfranchise Confederate leaders and make the abolition of slavery the law of the rebel states. He envisioned no other changes beyond these. His plan definitely excluded any guarantee of civil rights for the freedmen. By making the election law of 1860 the basis of the new electorate he not only excluded Negro suffrage, but would perpetuate the prevailing methods of legislative apportionment by which the slavemasters had maintained

political domination over the small-farming regions of
the state.* Without enfranchising the really democratic sections of the southern populace, the restrictions upon a few Confederate leaders would mean
nothing. No other class was present to seize the reins
of state power in the South. It was equivalent, as later
events showed, to restoring the former ruling class to
the seat of government.

Assuming that the power of reconstructing the states
belonged to him, Lincoln proceeded with his plan. Virginia he already considered reconstructed under the
shadowy Pierpont Government at Alexandria, which
had effected no essential reform. Early in 1864, the
plan was carried out in the loyal section of Louisiana.
A governor was elected and installed; a constitutional
convention passed an anti-slavery constitution which
was adopted by 16% of the voters of 1860. Arkansas
went through the same shadow-boxing and elected representatives to the House.

But by this time opposition was crystallizing. Events
in the South were beginning to assume a revolutionary
trend. Demands for Negro suffrage and for protection
of civil rights in the South were already penetrating
Congress. The House refused to admit the representatives elected by the "loyal" State of Arkansas. Both
Houses of Congress passed the Wade-Davis Bill which
treated the Southern states as rebellious communities
and authorized the President to appoint a provisional
governor for each. It also provided that state governments could be established only after the war was over
and then only when a majority of the *white* voters had
taken the oath of loyalty and voted a constitution

* In states where total population was the basis of apportionment, the plantation regions sent representatives to the legislature not only for their whites, but for their large number of
slaves as well. Where the Federal ratio was used, three-fifths of
the slave population was counted as a basis for representation.

which abolished slavery and repudiated the Confederate debt. This was far from being a clear statement of the revolutionary course, and the Bill did not receive the support of Stevens. But it would have placed the power of readmitting states in the hands of Congress and this was sufficient for Lincoln to veto the bill.

The principal issues were beginning to project themselves clearly. The cleavage was already so sharp that a split in the National Union Party (a combination of Conservative Republicans, Radical Republicans and War Democrats) was narrowly averted in the elections of 1864. As it was, the popular vote for Lincoln was no great victory: he received 2,330,552 votes and the Democratic candidate 1,835,985, although the vote in the electoral college stood 212 to 21. The Republicans had entered the election on a platform which did not commit them to any plan of Reconstruction. The principal emphasis was upon defeating the South. Confidence in Lincoln was reconfirmed, emancipation and the arming of Negroes supported. The Democrats, on the extreme Right, entered the election on a platform which called the war a failure and demanded a truce in preparation for a compromise with the Confederates. As long as the Civil War was still in progress, the election showed, it would be dangerous for the Republicans to split.

Nevertheless, when Congress convened in early December, it refused to recognize the electoral vote of Louisiana and Tennessee, reconstructed under Lincoln's plan, and thereby repudiated the plan itself.

The Thirteenth Amendment, prohibiting slavery in the United States and all its territories, was passed by Congress on January 31, 1865, and was ratified during the summer and autumn. Its ratification marked the end of the first stage of the revolution. A new phase now demanded new revolutionary measures. The Left parliamentary arm of the revolution was shortly to become formidable; the Center, hitherto represented by Lincoln, would swerve sharply to the Right.

Lee surrendered April 9, 1865; Lincoln was assassinated on April 14. For the new period now opening, Lincoln had established a plan of reconstruction which would lead to quick and easy restoration and the rapid legalization of counter-revolution in the South. "Well for his reputation that he did not live to execute it," said Stevens. "From being the most popular, he would have left office the most unpopular man that ever occupied the executive chair."

"Jefferson Davis Johnson"

THE odium of history fell instead upon Andrew Johnson, who had been given second place on the National Union Party ticket in the 1864 election as a representative of Southern Unionists and of War Democrats. In the political coalition which ruled the North during the war, he therefore stood further to the Right than Lincoln. Representing most directly the middle class elements of the South—who, despite their hatred of the slave master's power, stood closer to them than any other faction of the middle class—Johnson traveled quickly along the road towards reconciliation. He was driven in this direction by the rise of the industrial and financial oligarchy of the North. If the working class had been sufficiently developed to play an independent and weighty political rôle, another alternative might have presented itself to a middle class wedged between rising and falling oligarchies.

Johnson was keenly aware of the two opposing aristocracies pressing from right and left upon his class. He told an interviewer:

The aristocracy based on $3,000,000,000 of property in slaves south of Mason's and Dixon's line has disappeared, but an aristocracy, based on over $2,500,000,000 of national securities, has arisen in the Northern States to assume that political control which the consolidation of great financial and political interests formerly gave to the slave oligarchy of the late rebel states. The aristocracy based on Negro property disappears at the southern end of the line only to reappear in an oligarchy of bonds and national securities in the states which repressed the rebellion.[4]

In his hands the reconstruction policies inaugurated by Lincoln became the instrument of counter-revolution. "Jefferson Davis Johnson," Wendell Phillips dubbed him and there could have been no more appropriate nickname. A few weeks after he had taken over the office of President, Johnson issued his proclamation of amnesty and pardon which, with two notable exceptions, was similar to Lincoln's. He included among those forbidden to take the oath of loyalty all Confederates who had taxable property to the amount of $20,000 or over. If carried through, this clear class measure would have debarred the most powerful sector of the former ruling class in the South. But another provision, in which Johnson assumed power to pardon all those in the excepted classes upon special application to himself, offered the means of restoring political rights to most of the former Confederates. The machinery for administering the loyalty oath was made very simple, and, with a liberal use of the special pardon, Johnson proceeded to "reconstruct" the states on the basis of their old electorate and even their old leaders.

Before Congress met in December 1865, the Johnsonian restoration ruled in the South. Under provisional governors appointed by Johnson, constitutional conventions were elected on the basis of the old elec-

torate. The conventions met and "abolished slavery"
by amendment to the old constitutions; state governments were elected and representatives and senators
to Congress designated. Then Johnson, willy-nilly, proclaimed the war at an end and civil government in
operation in the former Confederacy, reserving the
right to resort to military control when necessary.

In his first annual message, the President bore the
glad tidings to Congress. Now all that was to be done
was to permit the former rebel states to ratify the
Thirteenth Amendment, which "being adopted, it will
remain for the states whose powers have been so long
in abeyance to resume their places in the two branches
of the National Legislature, and thereby complete the
work of restoration."

Restoration it was, not of free and democratic states
to the Union, but of the lords of manors and dukedoms
to political power in the South. "Now is the critical
time," warned Wendell Phillips. "The rebellion has not
ceased, it has only changed its weapons. Once it fought,
now it intrigues; once it followed Lee in arms, now it
follows President Johnson in guile and chicanery; once
its headquarters were in Richmond, now it encamps
in the White House."

"Hold the [Anti-Slavery] societies together," Sumner had written Phillips from Washington, "the crisis
is grave."

The task was still ahead. The Abolition forces, the
extreme Left of the bourgeois democracy, had to turn
their Anti-Slavery Society into an Anti-Restoration
sledge-hammer.

On the national arena, as well as in the South, revolution and counter-revolution faced each other on a
new plane of conflict.

CHAPTER II

FIGHTING FOR LAND

Land Seizures During the War

THE Federal soldiers who raided the countryside around Jackson, Mississippi, early in 1863, told the slaves on a large plantation that they were free and gave them guns. The Federals went on their way but the Negroes measured off the land with a plowline, making a fair apportionment among themselves, and also divided the cotton and farm implements. The "insurgent Negroes" were later captured by Confederate soldiers and brought into Jackson.

"This is only one instance of the wholesome effects of Abolitionism," declared the local newspaper. "Let the country be thus subjugated, and Lincoln's robbers will occupy every farm in the South." [1]

Although Lincoln did not see eye to eye with this Bourbon editor on the consequences of defeat, the Negro "robbers" were quite ready to fulfill his prophecy. Early they sensed the true path of revolution. The war had broken the chains of chattel slavery, had placed weapons in their hands. With a plowline, the Negroes on that Big Black plantation in Mississippi were charting the further course of revolution in the South.

And not only in Mississippi. Wherever Northern troops occupied plantation territory the same experience was repeated. In hundreds of instances, says one account, the "more insolent Negroes actually passed over their former masters' lands, measuring with old ropes and setting pegs to mark the favorite tracts they designed taking possession of as soon as the word was given." [2] With the insolence of revolution the untutored ex-slaves were proving themselves far better educated in the needs of the epoch than their Northern allies. In many instances they took possession of land dangerously near the field of battle, risking their liberty and even their lives. Along the North Carolina coast, when the Union Army had not captured enough ground to "rest their tents upon," freedmen squatted on lands outside of the towns and in "No Man's Land," and there grew cotton and corn or made turpentine. [3] In southeastern Virginia, former slave-breeding center, they settled on abandoned plantations, where they constructed cabins in which they dwelt until forcibly ejected. [4]

The basic issue of Reconstruction in the South was thus prominently projected even during the war. Emancipation and the arming of Negroes had been forced upon the North by the contingencies of war and by the pressure of tens of thousands of refugee slaves upon the Army camps. Again, events in the South, the inevitable outcome of victorious war, were insistently confronting the Northern party with the next step. Confiscation of the landed estates and their distribution among the freedmen would assure the most complete transformation of Southern society possible within the limits of capitalism (the revolution could not, and did not, go beyond those limits).

Like Emancipation, the first revolutionary step, confiscation and distribution of the land, would affect the Negroes most directly. The mass of non-slaveholding whites were small peasant proprietors in the hill country, where they had been driven by the expanding slave system, or on the less productive soil along the fringes of the plantations. Only few were landless, although many could boast only a few outworn acres and most of the "poor whites" were hungry for more land. Land redistribution would open the fertile regions to these white farmers also and expand their landholdings. But the chief beneficiaries would be the 4,000,000 freedmen on the plantations, whom the war had released as a vital force moving towards the seizure of the estates.

Confiscation of the plantations would assure the easiest and quickest consolidation of the Northern victory. At one stroke the bourgeoisie could deprive the former ruling class in the South of its economic power, destroy decisively the basis for a restoration, and provide in a large class of small farm-owners a solid base for bourgeois democracy to replace the slave oligarchy. But rarely do bourgeois revolutions follow this pattern. The Great French Revolution most closely approximated such a course. In Prussia, where the French Revolution inspired the abolition of serfdom from above, the old Junker estates remained as a basis for the new labor relationships on the land. In Russia, too, the peasantry remained dependent upon the landed estates after the emancipation of the serfs in 1861.

The outcome of the struggle for land would decide whether the new South would retain strong remnants of the old slave system based upon the plantations, or would enjoy rapid capitalist development unhampered by obstacles inherited from chattel slavery. What was done with the landed estates would solve this question. While the freedmen, in a spontaneous and unorganized manner, were pressing for a revolutionary solution, the bourgeoisie was already committing itself to a slow evolutionary course. At the outset the revolution was torn between the two paths.

Reform vs. Revolution on the Land Question

EARLY in the war, the North was already confronted with the necessity of choosing which course it would pursue on the land problem. As the Northern Army occupied Confederate territory, large tracts of abandoned plantations and stores of cotton fell into its hands. At the close of 1861, the Federals were already at Port Royal, S. C., the center of a rich cotton and rice area; early in 1862 they occupied the New Orleans region, and further up the Mississippi General Grant established himself at Grand Junction. Before Lincoln issued his Proclamation, slaves were proclaiming Emancipation by flocking into the Army camps from the surrounding country. But the plantations could not walk. Would the slaves return to them as free landowners or as forced laborers?

In the Confiscation Act of 1862 Congress placed a powerful revolutionary weapon in Lincoln's hands. The Act authorized the President "to cause the seizure of all the estates and property, money, stocks, credit and effects" of all military and civil officers of the Confederacy or of its states and after 60 days' notice to confiscate the property of all "engaged in armed rebellion" against the United States. Lincoln balked at the Act and expressed himself against any plan for wholesale and perpetual confiscation of "real estate." He approved the Bill only after he had informed Congress that he would be very chary in its application. Nevertheless, in the occupied areas the plantations abandoned by their owners and others, which had been confiscated from active supporters or officers of the Confederacy, were taken over by the Army commands.

In no instances were outright land grants given to the freedmen in the three areas then occupied. The Negroes were put to work on the abandoned land under

varying forms of wage-labor, forced labor and sometimes share-tenancy. Around Port Royal, each freedman was assigned two acres of land (with five-
sixteenths of an acre additional for each child) on
which he was to raise food for his own use. But in
payment for the use of the land and livestock, the
freedmen were to raise cotton for the government on
plantations set aside for this purpose. At New Orleans,
General Butler assigned a supervisor to take care of
the abandoned plantations and supplied the necessary
labor from the refugee camps, stipulating wages at $10
a month for first-class hands and the 10-hour day.
His successor, General Banks, made labor on public
works and elsewhere compulsory for Negroes who had
no means of support. General Grant ordered the freedmen to gather the crops on the plantations in western
Tennessee and cut timber on a wage basis. At the end
of 1863, the Treasury Department appointed agents
to organize freedmen's labor or "home" colonies on the
abandoned plantations for the purpose of raising cotton for the government and generally to supervise the
property left by fleeing slavemasters. The freedmen
were sometimes forced by the military to work in these
colonies under vague wage stipulations or on some
share-crop basis.[5]

These arrangements could be only temporary and
depended upon what was to be finally done with the
abandoned and confiscated lands. A precedent was
already being established by the military governors.
Some of the land was sold for taxes, and a few Negroes,
especially in the Port Royal area, were able to buy
small tracts. But most of the large plantations were
being leased out to private contractors, who exploited
the freedmen. Generals, Treasury Department agents
and Northern capitalists were also taking advantage
of the opportunity to buy up large tracts of land. Gov-

ernor Andrews of Massachusetts, the storm center of Abolition, invested $30,000 in a Mississippi plantation; Senator Sprague of Rhode Island was a heavy buyer of confiscated property in Florida; Colonel Butler, brother of the General, was favored with easy leases on the plantations in the sugar parishes near New Orleans. At Newbern, N. C., the large cotton plantations were leased to white men who employed 6,000 freedmen. Wages ranging from $5 to $10 a month were stipulated in the leases, but the workers were often swindled out of their wages. On the government-managed lands the freedmen were encountering their first experience of contract labor. Many refused to work because they expected that the lands would be given them.

Another tendency was also apparent during this period. In some places large plantations were assigned the former slaves with the understanding that Congress would confirm their title to the land. "The nest in which the rebellion was hatched has become the Mecca of Freedom," declared General Dana when he set aside the 10,000-acre plantation of Jefferson Davis, President of the Confederacy, as a home colony for the Negroes, under the protection of a Negro regiment.[6] In a number of home colonies the Negroes set up a form of self-government and in some places worked the land on a coöperative basis. At Davis Bend, Miss., the area was divided into districts each having a Negro sheriff and judge. "The Community distinctly demonstrated the capacity of the Negro," declared the officer in charge of Negro affairs for General Grant, "to take care of himself and exercise under honest and competent direction the functions of self-government."[7] When the Negro village of Mitchellville was created at Hilton's Head, S. C., provisions were made for compulsory education for all children between the ages of six and fifteen years.[8] Even before the armed combat reached a decisive conclusion, the former slaves were already reaching out eagerly for all the benefits of democracy.

The most far-reaching step towards the distribution of land was General Sherman's Special Field Orders No. 15,* issued with the acquiescence of the War Department on January 16, 1865. Sherman was then pursuing the remnants of the Confederate Army northward. An army of refugees, almost as large as the Army itself, had joined General Sherman's column on its famous march to the sea. The General authorized the freedmen to take possession of the land on the Sea Islands, off the coast between Charleston, S. C., and Jacksonville, Fla., and the abandoned rice plantations for thirty miles inland. Each freedman was granted possessory title over forty acres of land for the duration of the war, with the understanding that the land would be given them permanently by Congress. General Saxton, who was made Inspector of the settlements and plantations in this region, testified that in urging the Negroes to cross to the Sea Islands "the faith of the government was solemnly pledged to maintain them in possession."

In a short time 40,000 freedmen settled on the land and proceeded to work it as their own. On some of the islands the freedmen established civil government, with constitutions and laws for the regulation of their internal affairs, with all the different departments for schools, churches, building roads, and other improvements.[9] On one of the islands the Negro farmers within a few short months had carried through improvements amounting to a sum "large enough to have purchased the whole island three years ago, with all the improve-

* See Appendices, Document 1.

ments of 200 years under the rule and culture of its white inhabitants." [10]

General Sherman's order was to have reverberations for years to come; it turned the Sea Islands into the most advanced outpost of the revolution. Even here the Negroes were to retain their land only after a long and bitter struggle, but this first clear-cut, unequivocal action of their Northern ally with regard to land aroused and heartened the freedmen.

The bourgeoisie refused to take General Sherman's order as its springboard. A more or less uniform land policy was established in the Bill of March 1865, creating the Bureau of Refugees, Freedmen and Abandoned Lands (the Freedmen's Bureau) under the supervision of the War Department. The main purpose of the Bureau, which was set up in each Southern state under the direction of a Commissioner, was to manage the abandoned lands, supervise the labor relations of the freedmen with their employers, and extend temporary relief to refugees and former slaves. The Bill made it clear that redistribution of the land in the form of free grants to freedmen was not contemplated. Instead, the commissioners of the Bureau were authorized to assign to each freedman and "loyal white refugee" not more than forty acres of land from the abandoned and confiscated plantations. The land was to be leased for a term of three years at an annual rent of six percent of its value in 1860, when land prices were at their peak.

It was clear, then, that the Northern party did not intend to carry through any revolutionary land policy, that, at most, it would permit Negroes to rent land on the confiscated plantations which had not yet been leased to large contractors. No further measures were indicated and the land which the Bureau took over, amounting to about 800,000 acres, could hardly supply

4,000,000 landless peasants with enough land to build a cabin upon. Only further confiscation of all the large estates could supply the necessary land, but instead the Bureau sold most of its best land to large operators and to speculators and by 1868 it held title to only 140,000 acres of the worst land. Despite the cry of the Democrats that the people were being taxed to maintain idle and good-for-nothing Negroes and "poor whites," the Bureau collected enough rent, paid mostly by Negroes, during its first year to meet all its expenses.[11]

The Bureau's work in the South consisted almost entirely in the regulation of labor relations between the Negro and his employer and later it acted as a barrier against the functioning of the "Black Codes" passed by the Johnson Conventions. In the regulation of labor relations the Bureau was necessarily dominated by capitalist ideology. One Bourbon editor, commenting on an order of the Bureau which established wage scales at a maximum of $10 a month and provided for the 10-hour day and regular payment of wages, points out:

> On the other hand the Negro laborer is required to keep his part of the contract and to work faithfully, on penalty of being declared a vagrant and put to labor on some public works. . . . It would be well for the Negroes themselves, who can read this order, to do so, and for employers to keep a copy by them and read it to their employees.[12]

Widespread Agitation for Land

WHILE the bourgeoisie was undertaking a reform course on the issue of land and would have preferred to keep the old land relationships, the Negro masses made their demands heard in no uncertain terms. They refused to accept the long-term labor contracts (which the Freedmen's Bureau negotiated for them with the large planters), sharecropping or similar arrangements which smacked too much of the old slavery. They wanted the land and fully expected that it would be given them.

How certain the former slaves were that the land would be theirs is clear from all accounts of the period. Sidney Andrews, correspondent in the South for the Boston *Advertiser* and the Chicago *Tribune,* reported after an extended trip in 1865:

There is among the plantation Negroes a widely spread idea that land is to be given them by the government, and this idea is at the bottom of much idleness and discontent. ... The Negroes almost universally believe that the islands [Sea Islands] have been given to them, and they are not likely to readily relinquish that belief ... an attempt to force them from the islands at present, or to compel them to the acceptance of the terms proposed by the planters, will overthrow their faith in the government, and there will be—bloodshed.[13]

Similar testimony is offered by Whitelaw Reid, a Conservative Republican journalist on the New York *Tribune.* Writing about the freedmen's reaction to the plan, then widely discussed, of colonizing them in Liberia, he said: "They believe in colonization, but it is colonization of the lands they have been working. From the bare idea of forced, or even voluntary removal to other sections they utterly revolt." [14]

The editor of a Democratic paper in North Carolina was alarmed at "the universality of the impression among the Negroes that there will be a division of the lands of their former masters among them on the first of January." He noted that newspapers throughout the South were full of accounts of such expectations and concluded that: "Accident might account for the prevalence of such a belief in any particular locality, but it is observable that the folly is as widespread as the race itself." [15]

The presence of armed Negroes—regiments and militias—made the land agitation more than mere folly. Our North Carolina editor was correct: where there were plantations there were freedmen wanting them. From Texas to Virginia the press reported that freedmen were preparing insurrections if they did not receive land by January 1, 1866. Although no wide-scale insurrections developed, these reports reflect the high state of tension in the plantation country and indicate clearly that land was the central question. "A man of much apparent intelligence informed me," wrote Andrews, "that the Negroes have an organized military force in all sections of the State [South Carolina], and are almost certain to rise and massacre the whites at Christmas time." The former slaveholders were living in perpetual fear of Negro uprisings.[16]

The reports of the Commissioners in charge of the Freedmen's Bureau in the South run along similar lines. "Unfortunately," the Commissioner of Georgia informed Congress, "there is a widespread belief among the people of this State that at Christmas time there is to be a distribution of property among them, and under this impression they are refusing to make contracts for the coming year." From Virginia came similar news and the Commissioner hastened to add that the "superintendents and agents of this bureau will take the earliest opportunity to explain to the freedmen that no lands will be given to them by the government." [17] General Swayne, Alabama Commissioner, issued a circular informing the Negroes they need not hope that plantations are to be parceled out among them and telling them that they "must go to work and behave themselves." [18]

Rôle of Negro Troops

THE presence of armed Negroes and of Federal troops meant that there was at hand the wherewithal for insurrection and the seizure of land. The elements were present: the owners of estates had been defeated in war; a section of the landless Negro masses had arms and could count for support upon at least a section of the Federal soldiers. Organization and leadership was lacking, but a series of spontaneous actions could force the Northern bourgeoisie to take decisive and positive action.

The more advanced among the soldiers, both white and Negro, were counseling direct action. A reporter of the New York *Nation* was shocked at the direct manner in which the freedmen tended to fulfill the basic demands of the revolution. "In the best of our regiments," he complained, "there are a few mischief makers who persuade the field hands that they should refuse to work, that they are the rightful owners of the land." The commander of a Negro regiment at Jackson (Miss.) told landless Negroes that they must defend their rights "to the click of the pistol, and at the point of the bayonet." Senator Lamar of Mississippi reported in December 1865 that planters from the surrounding country came into Vicksburg "in great fear," saying that the Negroes were arming and demanding lands by Christmas, or they would take them by force.[19]

News of the arming of Negroes and of their insurrectionary intentions at this time may have been exaggerated by the Southern press to justify the extreme reactionary measures undertaken during the second half of 1865 by the Johnson governments. But the persistence of such reports from all parts of the South and from varied sources indicates that a mass move-

ment was rapidly shaping itself. Two North Carolina
gentlemen from different counties testified that the
"white citizens had all been deprived of arms, while the
Negroes were almost all of them armed by some means
or other." [20] In a report to President Johnson, B. C.
Truman said that from the surrender of the rebel
armies up to the Christmas holidays of 1865 the South
had "terrible fears of a servile insurrection.... In one
way or another they have procured great numbers of
army muskets and revolvers... there were extensive
seizures of arms and ammunition, which the Negroes
had foolishly collected, and strict precautions were
taken to avoid any outbreak." [21]

So active a rôle did the regular Negro troops play
in the agitation for land and civil rights that President
Johnson was flooded with appeals for their withdrawal.
General Grant, who took a short trip into the South
on the request of the President, and who gathered
most of his material from the former ruling class, urged
in December 1865 that only white troops be maintained
in the South for "obvious reasons," the most important
being that the Negro troops, lately slaves, "demoral-
ize labor, both by their advice and by furnishing in
their camps a resort for the freedmen for long distance
round." The General discovered that the ex-slave
seemed "to be imbued with the idea that the property
of his late master should by right belong to him, or at
least should have no protection from the colored soldier." [22] A correspondent of President Johnson in
Florida wrote that especially where Negro troops were
stationed, the Negroes were "lazy, idling, thievish and
impudent." They seem to have been impudent enough
to want the land: "There is really danger of an insurrection that would surprise you if you were aware of
it, raised principally from the secret admonitions of
colored troops." [23]

Governor Humphreys of Mississippi complained to President Johnson that Negro troops "did infinite mischief by misrepresenting the purpose and intentions of the State government," in advising the freedmen not to work for their late masters since the lands would be divided among them. Finally the Governor sent a commission to Washington to explain the danger of insurrection among the Negro troops and to procure arms for a state militia.[24]

The Reactionary Holiday

THE years 1865-1866 were crucial. This was the point at which the bourgeoisie could have taken a decisive step in the direction of a revolutionary solution of the land problem. Instead, a reactionary holiday was inaugurated by President Johnson. The revolution had to hold its breath and even retreat, pending the outcome of the struggle of the industrial bourgeoisie, as represented by the Radical Republicans, for political hegemony in the Republic. The great and violent battles in Congress were just beginning and a decisive outcome was not to occur until 1867. In the meantime, reaction in the South set in.

A few months after Johnson had been in office, Marx already was writing Engels (June 24, 1865):

Johnson's policy disturbs me. Laughable affectation of force against certain individuals; until now highly vacillating and weak in practice. The reaction has already begun in America and will soon become much stronger if the slovenliness existing up to now is not stopped.

The reaction, however, did not continue on a straight line. Another period of revolution was to intervene. In his reply to Marx's letter Engels pointed out that "without colored suffrage nothing can be done, and the decision of the question Johnson leaves to the defeated ex-slaveholders." He saw that the revolution must still complete its second lap:

However—he added—it must be counted upon that things will develop differently than the Mr. Barons imagine. . . . The oligarchy is going to its doom finally, but the process could be now quickly finished at one stroke, while it is being prolonged.[25]

During the early period of the Civil War, when Engels, "seeing only the military aspects of things," was highly disgusted with the progress of the revolution, Marx had written him that the situation at that time was "at most a kind of reaction that arises in every revolutionary movement." [26] Now, too, Johnson's reactionary holiday (Presidential Reconstruction, 1865-1867) was to give way before a revolutionary resurgence (Congressional Reconstruction, 1867-1876).

But during this intervening period of reaction, the ex-slaveholders were returning to power in the South. The Constitutional Conventions held towards the end of 1865 in the Southern states under Johnson's reconstruction plan were dominated by the old Confederate leaders. These Conventions accepted as a political expediency the emancipation of the Negroes, but for practical purposes passed the notorious "Black Codes" which were intended to restore forced labor conditions on the plantations. The spirit of the dominant Bourbon wing of these Conventions is expressed in the words of a Florida planter: "If the slaves are freed by the proclamation the nigger will still be their slave in some way." [27]

The Conventions set about refining chattel slavery with a vengeance. The ferocity of the Black Codes can be explained only by the ferment on the countryside. They were intended to still the gathering revolutionary storm in the Black Belt and stifle the striving of the ex-slaves for land and political freedom. The Black Codes can be compared with the vagrancy acts of Western Europe at the end of the 15th and through the 16th centuries. Due to the breaking up of the feudal estates of Western Europe, a large body of future proletarians were cut loose from the land and from their masters. Industry, however, could not yet absorb them and the vagrancy laws were used to imprison and put to forced labor this large landless and jobless mass. In the South, 4,000,000 Negro slaves had become masterless. There was no industry to absorb them; they were propelled instead towards seizing the large landed estates. Counter-revolution replied with the Black Codes, consisting of vagrancy and apprenticeship acts designed to force Negroes to labor on the plantations under conditions imposed by the planters.

We will describe only one law, called curiously enough an "Act to Confer Civil Rights on Freedmen and for other purposes," passed by the Mississippi Convention in November 1865, as typical of the Black Codes in the other states. The rights conferred upon Negroes were strictly limited: the right to hold and dispose of personal property, to sue and be sued in the courts of the State, and the recognition of marriage among Negroes. For the rest, the law would not permit Negroes to rent lands or houses except in incorporated towns or cities and then only under the control of the corporate authorities; forbade intermarriage between white and Negro; every Negro had to show a license from police or a written labor contract to prove employment; any Negro quitting a job could be arrested; any one "enticing" a Negro from employment or employing a "deserter" from a contract or aiding him in any way was guilty of a misdemeanor. No Negro, unless in the Army, was permitted to keep or carry weapons or ammunition. Any Negro "committing riots, affrays, trespasses, malicious mischief ... seditious speeches, insulting gestures, language or acts" could be fined and imprisoned. And finally, so as to make the meaning completely clear, the laws under chattel slavery were declared again in full force "except so far as the mode and manner of trial and punishment have been changed or altered by law."

In a number of states the commissioners of the Freedmen's Bureau ordered the Black Codes repealed or would not permit them to be carried out, although there is evidence that the vagrancy and apprenticeship laws were partially effective until their repeal by the Constitutional Conventions of 1868 and the new Reconstruction Legislatures. As the Bureau stated in a list of grievances submitted to Congress, the Black Codes "actually served to secure to the former slaveholding class the unpaid labor which they had been accustomed to enjoy before the war." [28] General Terry, in charge of the Department of Virginia, ordered civil officers to prohibit the enforcement of the Codes and declared that their "ultimate result will be to reduce the freedmen to the condition of servitude worse than that from which they have been emancipated." [29]

The passage of the Black Codes by the Conventions proved that Johnson was restoring the old ruling class in the South. These were the "reconstructed" states which Johnson, in his first annual message, urged Congress to restore to the Union.

But the Black Codes also indicate the sharpness of the struggle which was proceeding in the South. Their whole force was directed against the attempts of the former slaves to acquire the land and to establish some degree of free labor.

Johnson was also using freely the special power of pardon which he had assumed in his proclamation of amnesty. Every pardon carried with it an order to restore the confiscated property. This, however, was not an easy task. As long as Negroes were armed and Negro regiments were stationed in the plantation areas, an attempt to restore confiscated plantations on which Negroes were working as lessees or upon which they had squatted would be a bloody process. Johnson was again appealed to by the South to recall the Negro troops. The Legislature of Alabama on January 16, 1866, sent the following memorial to the President:

The freedmen of this State, the great majority of whom are under contracts for labor for the present year, yielding to the natural credulity characteristic of the race, cherish the belief that their idleness, violation of contracts, and insubordination are indirectly countenanced by the soldiers, and most especially by the colored portions of them. A vague and indefinite idea pervades the masses of freedmen, that at the expiration of the present year [1866] a general division of property will be made among them. It is believed that this state of mind is produced by their frequent intercourse and association with the colored troops. It is needless to remind your Excellency that while this groundless and ridiculous delusion continues, the agricultural and industrial interests must suffer, while at the same time the evils and horrors of domestic insurrection may be reasonably anticipated.[30]

Appeals such as these found a ready response from the President. On April 2, 1866, Johnson declared that in the "insurrectionary states the law can be sustained and enforced by the proper civil authorities." A number of regiments were withdrawn from the field; attempts were made to disarm and disband the Negro militias.

Chattel slavery, however, was now definitely a thing of the past. The former slavemasters could hope only to retain the plantations on which the former slaves could be forced to work under semi-feudal conditions. The enlightened paternalism of the ex-slaveholders was expressed neatly by the president of the reactionary Georgia Convention: "Our conduct should be kind, magnanimous, just.... We may indulge a hope that we may organize them [the Negroes] into a class of trustworthy laborers." [31]

Struggle on the Sea Islands

THE gentleman was to find it a trying task, indeed. The Negroes did not wish to become "trustworthy laborers," and continued their struggle for land. While the bourgeoisie did not support them on this fundamental demand, Freedmen's Bureau agents and Army officers, who opposed the governments set up by Johnson, sometimes came to their aid. It was a struggle, however, in which the Negroes had to face the enemy almost alone, even hampered by the insistence of the Freedmen's Bureau on carrying through the labor contracts with the employers.

In many places the Negro farmers refused to return the confiscated plantations to the former owners. The struggle on the Sea Islands was the most dramatic and prolonged. When the planters, who had been pardoned by the President, came to claim their plantations, the Negroes armed themselves with every available weapon. One Negro leader told the former slavemasters: "You had better go back to Charleston, and go to work there, and if you can do nothing else, you can pick oysters and earn your living as the loyal people have done—by the sweat of their brows." [32] The Bureau agents refused to release the land and asked Congress to confirm the titles of the Negroes as had been promised when the land was originally given them. General Howard, head of the Bureau, was dis-

patched from Washington to try to pacify the freedmen and turn the land over to the former slavemasters.
The Negroes were angry and felt that the government
had deceived them. They refused to abide by a compromise agreement which would permit them to gather
the crop and which provided for schools, because the
plan recognized the ownership of their former masters.
The Negroes were in possession and did not permit the
former owners to place foot on the land.[33]

The following dispatch in Garrison's *Liberator*, from
Charleston, S. C., December 9, 1865, shows how persistently the Negroes were fighting to retain the land:

On Edisto Island, the Negroes, incensed at the restoration
of the land to their former owners, refuse to enter into
contracts with them. Many of the plantations are, therefore, offered for rent at reasonable rates. Brevet Brigadier
General Buche has recently been sent to the island to prevent disturbances, and has issued an order forbidding all
persons from visiting the island without proper passes, and
offering a guard from his headquarters to former owners
who desire to attempt overtures to their workmen.

Note the strict censorship on visits to the island;
there were people on the mainland helping the island
dwellers in their struggle against the former masters.
Note also that none of the former slaveowners dared
visit the island unless accompanied by a guard!

Governor Aiken, in company with some officers of our
army, visited on Thursday last his rice plantations on
Jehossee Island, in order to attempt some arrangement for
work during the coming season. The Negroes utterly refused
to come to any terms, and begged an officer of General
Sickles' staff, who was with the party, to "see de gubber-
mint, and ax him if he wouldn't sell de land, and leff um to
pay sum udder time, an ef we dont pay in two year, den
he may take um back." Unwilling to give up that hope of
lands which has its birth in General Saxton's measures and

General Sherman's colonization order, these poor people declare their determination to "work for no rebels." [34]

Congress was finally obliged to take some action. The Bill extending the life of the Freedmen's Bureau for another year (which was passed over Johnson's veto on July 16, 1866) made provisions for settlement of the land dispute on the Sea Islands. It confirmed the early sales made to Negroes in South Carolina around Port Royal; those who had been given leases on confiscated lands were granted full ownership. The tax lands held by the United States in this area, amounting to 38,000 acres, were ordered sold at $1.50 an acre to the Negroes holding land under Sherman's field order and what lands remained were to be sold to those Negroes who held land but were dispossessed by the return of the former owner. Freedmen who claimed land under Sherman's order were to be given a lease on twenty acres of government-owned land in South Carolina for six years at the end of which period they could buy the land at $1.50 an acre. Finally, the Bill provided that lands shall not be restored to their former owners until the growing crop is taken in by the freedmen at present on the land. [35]

This is the furthest the bourgeoisie went towards distribution of land. Only in some instances was outright ownership recognized; in general the principle of purchase prevailed, although the price was low enough to enable some freedmen to obtain land. Even this action by Congress came only after the Negro masses had maintained their possession "illegally" and was merely the recognition of an accomplished fact, although pains were taken not to leave the impression that the land was being distributed free.

But the struggle did not end here. In the same Bill Congress recognized the title to land of the previous masters who had returned to claim the plantations. The Negroes refused to give up this land, which was only nominally in the hands of the former owners. In January 1867 another incident occurred which shows the temper of the Negro peasants. The theoretical owner of the Delta Plantations, one of the largest tracts of land in the area, had leased the plantation to an ex-Confederate officer, with whom the Negroes refused to deal. The officer called upon the Freedmen's Bureau to eject the Negroes. A corporal and five soldiers proceeded to the plantation to enforce the order of the commanding general that Negroes holding no possessory titles were to be compelled either to make contracts with the new lessee or else leave the plantation and proceed to St. Helena, where twenty acres of land would be granted them by the government.

These terms were rejected by the Negroes and when the corporal tried to enforce them he was surrounded by 200 freedmen, armed with muskets, pistols, clubs and missiles of every kind, "some of them swearing that they would die rather than contract with Captain Barnwell or depart for St. Helena Island." Why, indeed, should they, after having built all kinds of improvements on the plantation with full expectation of having it as their own?

The soldiers were forced to leave the plantation. A well-armed detail of 50 men, provided with three day's rations, was then dispatched by the commanding general. "It was supposed that the appearance of so large a military force would have the effect of intimidating the refractory Negroes, and thus force them into obedience without the useless shedding of blood. Arriving on the island it was found that the entire population was carefully picketed _à la militaire_." A parley was held in which the Bureau officer told the Negroes that they had no title to the land. "But the parley produced

no better results, and, if anything, tended to increase
the anger of the freedmen, who crowded together in
solid phalanx, and swore more furiously that they
would die where they stood before they would surrender their claims to the land. One of the leaders
remarked, 'We have but one master now—Jesus Christ
—and he'll never come here to collect taxes or drive
us off.'"

The Negro squatters were ready to fight. "Fall in,
guards!" shouted their leader and the armed Negroes
drew up for battle. The Army officers thought it ad-
visable to withdraw their troops.[36]

In persistent and heroic struggles of this kind the
Negroes were able to hold on to the land. The final outcome of the struggle in the Sea Island area is shown
by the fact that in 1910 almost 60 percent of the
Negro farmers in the counties of Beaufort and Charleston owned their farms, in distinct contrast to the rest
of the plantation area in the South where a Negro farm
owner is a rarity.

Sporadic Battles for Land

The Sea Island experience was repeated on a lesser
scale and with less success in other parts of the South.
Despite the action of the Johnson régime and the reactionary Conventions, the landless Negro peasantry
clung tenaciously to the idea that the land belonged to
them. We find, for example, that at a public meeting
of freedmen in Greensboro, Ala., in December 1865,
called to elect delegates to a state-wide convention, the
demand for land was heard in no uncertain terms and
speakers declared that they would have "lands or
blood." [37]

Actions of the Negro masses were necessarily sporadic
and scattered. Bloody clashes, denounced by the lib-

erals as massacres of defenseless Negroes and described
in the Bourbon press as riots of ignorant and misled
blacks, became common. Although these clashes did
often prove to be massacres (in Alabama alone during
December 1865 and the first three months of 1866,
1,400 cases of assaults upon freedmen were brought before the Freedmen's Bureau), they were nevertheless
open and unconcealed struggles over land and political
rights.

The freedmen had faith in the North. Leaders of
500 Negroes who were accused of planning to seize
the large plantations near Memphis, Tennessee, and
some of whom were killed in the attempt, declared, for
instance, that if the freedmen would but take possession of the land their friends in Memphis and in the
North would stand by them.[38] But it became clearer
as the year wore on that the North had no intention
of dividing the lands, and that Northern military
authorities in the South were being employed to halt
land seizures. The first terror organizations, such as the
"Black Cavalry"—forerunners of the K.K.K.—were
formed during this period by the planters to protect
their lands and in many cases the Federal military
overlooked the formation of these armed militias of
the counter-revolution.

Northern troops, in fact, were actually putting down
Negro peasant insurrections. Near Richmond, Virginia,
a large military force was called upon to put down
"sedition" when a body of 500 Negroes, armed and
drawn up in line of battle, refused to pay rents on a
large plantation, claiming that they had a right to the
land.[39] The *Savannah Republican* tells of the "Ogee-
chee Negro Rebellion" involving, "it is variously estimated, from five to twelve hundred armed men" whose
aim was to take possession of the plantations near
Savannah. Officers of the law were arrested and driven

out of the district and the highways were patrolled by
Negro guards. With the consent of the Washington
authorities a large body of troops took possession of
the territory and put down the rebellion.[40] In other
places, as in Virginia, when the Negroes realized that
they had depended upon the North in vain, they
destroyed the fencing and other improvements upon
the plantations before releasing them.[41]

Through the whole period of Reconstruction the
demand for land was to run like a refrain. If freedom
meant anything it meant land and the vote. The revolution revolved around these points for a decade. Every
year there were reports of "Negro insurrections and
conspiracies" for the seizure of the land. The Republicans in the South continued to make ambiguous
promises about dividing the land in order to retain the
support of the agrarian masses. But when they designated the next and the next Christmas as the time of
division they were met with an increasing chorus of
shouts: "Division now; don't wait until Christmas;
we want it now!" [42] During the presidential elections
of 1868, many of the Negro farm workers were given
to understand that the election of Grant would be
equivalent to a homestead. We find the Governor of
Mississippi again warning the Negroes in 1867 that the
"first outbreak against the peace and quiet of the
State would signalize the destruction of their cherished
hopes and the ruin of their race." [43] Even as late as
1874, when reaction was practically in the saddle again
in the South, armed Negro militias persisted in attempts to seize land.

But the historical opportunity for general confiscation of the large landholdings and the distribution of
the lands had been missed. The crucial years were
1865-1866, when, as Charles Sumner realized, the
former slaveowners "were submissive. There was noth-

ing they would not do, even to the extent of enfranchising their freedmen and providing for them
homesteads." Events such as the Sea Islands episode
were showing that the wide-scale confiscation of the
land by the emancipated Negroes would have altered
the outcome of the revolution. But historical development had not yet ripened the Negro people to the
stage where they could independently carry through
this basic revolutionary step on a large and conclusive
scale. For the Negroes did not yet have a class among
them capable of independently leading the agrarian
revolution through to its end. The free Negro working
class was small, scattered in the cities of the North
and South, still in its swaddling clothes. No less in-
cipient was the Negro bourgeoisie. A small Negro
middle class supplied ministers, teachers, journalists,
lawyers who played an important part in the political
leadership of the Negro people during Reconstruction.
But the mass of Negroes were freedmen, just emancipated from chattel slavery, landless and propertyless,
as yet organizationally inarticulate, in motion but need-
ing a clear class leadership which would channelize the
mass energy in the direction of the fulfillment of their
basic needs.

The only class able to supply decisive revolutionary
leadership in this period was the industrial section of
the bourgeoisie. But during the crucial years it was
engaged primarily in winning political power for itself
on a national scale. In the meantime, two years of
petty-bourgeois vacillation in the North, typified by
the alliance of President Johnson with the Bourbons,
had permitted the former slaveowners to retain their
plantations and to regain those which had been confiscated. The revolution never again reached the point
where wholesale confiscation was even seriously considered.

Confiscation Defeated

REVOLUTIONARY bourgeois leaders, such as Stevens and Sumner, made proposals for a division of the land, but these were not well received by the Radical Republicans. Stevens' proposal, however, is of interest because it shows with what consistency he pursued the aims of the bourgeois revolution. For more than a year before the close of the war he had been talking of wholesale confiscation, and after the defeat of the Confederacy he returned to the subject often in his public addresses. He opposed violently any plan to colonize the freedmen in a place like Liberia, as had been suggested by Lincoln, and held that they should be provided for on the soil where they worked. He also opposed the return of the confiscated property to the former owners, declaring before the House (February 18, 1867) that "more than $2,000,000,000 of property belonging to the United States, confiscated not as rebel but as enemy property had been given back to enrich traitors."

Stevens computed that the Southern states and about 70,000 people owned 394,000,000 acres of land in the South and that a remaining 71,000,000 acres were owned by persons each of whom had less than 200 acres. He would permit the small owners to retain their land. But he would divide the estates of the "leading rebels" into tracts of 40 acres for each adult freedman. And the remainder would be sold to pay off the large national debt caused by the war. In this way, Stevens pointed out, the freedmen would be adequately taken care of, the "rebels" would be made to pay for their "treason," the huge national debt would not burden the people, "and yet nine-tenths of the people [in the South] would remain untouched."

These revolutionary proposals were incorporated in a Bill which the "Old Commoner" introduced into the House in March 1867, almost a year before his death. Besides providing each head of a family with 40 acres the Bill would also appropriate $50 to each for a homestead. He introduced it as his own measure since he was unable to obtain the support of the Republican Party for the Bill.

If we are to believe a Bourbon editor of Georgia, Stevens sent his private agents into the South to gain support for the measure. One of them, signing himself in code, is said to have written him from Virginia that he had "done a splendid business, having organized seven camps of the Grand Army which are recruiting rapidly. The objects, as I explain them (privately, of course) take amazingly, and I believe, sir, if all our agents would follow my plan, we would be safe in allowing reconstruction immediately. I tell them that our plan of confiscation is only to affect the large landowners, to compel them to divide their large bodies of land, say, into fifty or 150 acre farms; these farms to be sold to all classes of persons in the South only." In South Carolina and Georgia other agents also are said to have reported "a good business." [44]

Sumner introduced a series of resolutions in the Senate demanding other guarantees in the Reconstruction of the South, among them that "a homestead must be secured to the freedmen so that at least every head of a family may have a piece of land."

The colleagues of Stevens and Sumner were in no mood to listen to such pleas. They were engaged at the moment in another form of expropriation—the expropriation of the farmers of the West and even of the South for the benefit of the railroad and mining companies. Millions of acres of public lands were being

freely donated to the railroads,* and the farmers who
had staked claims under the Homestead Act along the
right of way found themselves suddenly dispossessed.
The New Orleans and Opelousas Railroad, for instance,
was at that time asking for an extension of the land
grant made before the war. Many of the small farmers
living on these railroad lands, as well as freedmen who
had settled on this only piece of free public property
available in the State, were ejected by the railroad. "It
seems to me very inconsistent for a Congress that
talked of confiscating plantations for the benefit of the
freedmen," wrote a New Orleans Radical Republican,
"to give away the only available land to a company of
speculators under the pretext that Northern capitalists
are interested in it." Northern capital had also invested
in the Alabama and Tennessee River railroads and the
Decatur and Nashville Road and others. Many of the
Republican leaders in the South were participating in
the land speculations and were opposed to giving the
land to the Negroes, while others were lessees and
owners of large plantations. "It is the Northern capitalist as well as the Southern planter that the poor
freedman has to contend against now," concluded the
observer in New Orleans.[45]

While the revolutionary tide was to rise again, new
forms of exploitation were crystallizing on the plantations. But the scales were already definitely tipped

---

* During the 'fifties and 'sixties, western railroad promoters received 158,293,000 acres of land from the Federal government.
Of this amount, 115,832,000 acres were actually certified and
patented. Railroad entrepreneurs likewise received land bounties
from individual states, amounting to 167,832,000 acres. It has
been estimated that the public lands, donated to the railroad
promoters, were worth $335,000,000, a sum equal to one-fifth of
the cost incurred in constructing the railroad domain of the
nation as it existed in 1870. In addition to the land bounties,
Federal, state and local governments contributed $707,100,000 in
direct money grants to the railroads.

against a revolutionary revision of the land relationships. Slowly, against the opposition of the Negro masses, the plantation system began to develop the characteristics that distinguish it today. Share-cropping, the transitory stage between chattel slavery and free wage-labor, was becoming the recognized and "ideal" relationship. The freedmen resisted sharply. "I am offering them even better terms than I did last year," complained a large plantation owner, "but nothing satisfies them. Grant them one thing and they demand something more, and there is no telling where they will stop." [46]

The prevalence of plans for inducing immigration from Europe and migration from the North at this time reflects the extremely unsettled status on the plantations and the refusal of the Negroes to submit to conditions but slightly different than chattel slavery. Attempts were made to obtain Irish immigrants, labor agencies were set up abroad, plans were drawn up for importing Chinese coolies, but without result. The immigrants found far better conditions in the North and those who came South were quick to leave. "All around us," complains a maternal Bourbon, "people are discussing how to get other laborers in place of the Negroes. But alas! ... I think things look very gloomy for the planters." [47]

Slowly and with great difficulty the Negroes were forced back upon the plantations under labor contracts, or as tenants and share-croppers.[48]

Defeated on the key issue of the revolution, the Negro people were handicapped from the start in the struggle for democratic rights. "Without confiscation, the result of Negro suffrage will slip through their fingers," declared a sage Bourbon editor.[49] When the bourgeoisie lent a deaf ear to the cry for land, the fate of democracy in the South was already sealed.

CHAPTER III

VICTORY OF THE LEFT

The Negro People's Conventions

WHILE the bourgeoisie was still crystallizing a revolutionary leadership to cope with the tasks of Reconstruction, the freedmen were already entering upon the battle for democracy. During the Johnsonian breathing spell, the Bourbon reaction was attempting to restore the pre-war relationships as nearly as possible without formal chattel slavery. A number of Johnson legislatures ratified the anti-slavery amendment to the Constitution of the United States on condition that Congress undertake no legislation with regard to the political status of the freedmen. In the South Carolina body a determined effort was even made to obtain compensation for freeing the slaves, and the governor was authorized to appoint a commission to hasten the recovery of confiscated lands. The personnel of the new state governments was substantially the same as it had been in 1861.

An organized movement against the Johnson governments and the Black Codes was initiated by the Negro conventions which met in the Southern states during the summer and fall of 1865. These conventions represented the first concerted political action by the Negro people in the South. As a whole they defined clearly and sharply the democratic issues of the revolution. The first to meet was at Nashville, Tennessee, in August 1865, under the chairmanship of a Negro barber of that city. Its resolutions insisted that

Congress recognize the rights of Negroes as citizens of the Republic, just as it had "recognized the rights and humanity of the black men" when it called for their assistance in putting down the rebellion of the slaveowners. They demanded that Tennessee representatives be barred from Congress unless the state legislature recognize the rights of the Negroes.[1]

In North Carolina the first freedmen's convention met at Raleigh in September 1865. Its 120 delegates from all parts of the State had to overcome stiff Bourbon opposition and many of them came at great risk to themselves. Some left their homes secretly at night and returned quietly after sunset; others received safe-conduct papers from the military authorities. "It is worth remarking," wrote the newspaper correspondent Andrews, "that it is really a convention of colored men, not a colored men's convention engineered by white men." Most of the delegates were freedmen, plantation hands, "dressed in the very cheapest of homespuns, awed by the very atmosphere of the city." John H. Harris, the leader of the convention, was a former slave "who did his daily task with other farm Negroes, and sat for hours, year in and year out, after that task was accomplished, in the fireplace, with a pine knot in one hand and a book in another; who is, in the true sense, self-educated; an upholsterer by trade, and, latterly, a teacher by profession."[2]

Like so many of the political bodies that were to follow in the South, this convention was primarily agrarian, with a sprinkling of city artisans and free Negroes. This convention of ex-slaves rejoiced over the passage of the anti-slavery amendment, the recognition of Haiti and Liberia by the United States, the admission of a Negro lawyer to the state courts. But the delegates did not merely rejoice over past gains; they demanded cash wages for labor, free education for their children, protection of the family relation and the repeal of discriminatory legislation. The convention pledged its support to Stevens, Sumner and other Radical Republicans in "their efforts to obtain equal political rights for all men." [3]

Similar conventions took place in other Southern states. The conventions in the deep South, in the very stronghold of the Bourbon power, were even bolder and raised more sharply the demands of the freedmen. The Colored People's Convention of South Carolina, meeting in Charleston in November 1865, defined clearly the stake of the Negro people in the revolution. In a petition to the reactionary State Legislature, the Convention demanded the repeal of the Black Codes, which had just been enacted, the right to serve on juries and testify in court, and the right of suffrage. These, said the resolution, "are the rights of free men, and are inherent and essential in every republican form of government."

The key political issues were most clearly formulated in a Memorial to the Senate of the United States.* By way of defense against the Black Codes, the Memorial asked for protection of life and property of all people and that the laborer be "as free to sell his labor as the merchant his goods." Above all it demanded that "a fair and impartial construction be given to the pledges of the government to us concerning the land question." This demand had direct bearing upon the situation in the Sea Islands, where the returning Confederates, pardoned by President Johnson, were attempting to regain the plantations held by the freedmen.

All the democratic rights were demanded:

We ask that the three great agents of civilized society— the school, the pulpit, the press—be as secure in South

* See Appendices, Document 2.

Carolina as in Massachusetts or in Vermont. We ask that
equal suffrage be conferred upon us, in common with the
white men of this State. . . . We ask that colored men shall
not in every instance be tried by white men; and that
neither by custom nor enactment shall we be excluded from
the jury box.

The document requested "the right to assemble in
peaceful convention, to discuss the political questions
of the day; the right to enter upon all the avenues of
agriculture, commerce, trade; to amass wealth by thrift
and industry." The delegates also adopted a vigorous
resolution for free education for white and Negro alike.

But the Convention suffered from no illusion about
the peaceful attainment of these rights as long as the
former rulers were permitted to hold power. It protested to Congress against the effort of the State Legislature to disarm the Negroes and demanded that they
be permitted to retain their weapons.[4] How well the
delegates realized that only the armed people could be
effective against the restoration and could guarantee
the rights of the Negro!

The demands cover the whole gamut of bourgeois
rights, from suffrage to private property and the right
to bear arms. This Memorial bears the stamp of the
bourgeois democratic revolution more legibly than any
other document produced by it.

The Convention realized full well the historic occasion. "An extraordinary meeting, unknown in the
history of South Carolina," it characterized itself in a
resolution, "when it is considered who compose it and
for what purposes it was allowed to assemble." Among
its delegates were people destined to play a leading
political rôle in the reconstruction of the State—Robert
C. DeLarge, A. J. Ransier, J. J. Wright, Beverly Nash,
Francis L. Cardozo, M. R. Delaney and Richard H.
Cain.

The Freedmen's Convention which gathered in Augusta, Georgia, in January 1866, created a permanent organization known as the Georgia Equal Rights Association, which was subsequently organized on a county basis throughout the State. The object of the Association, a Preamble declared, was "to secure for every citizen, without regard to race, descent or color, equal political rights." An Address to the State Legislature ran very much along the lines of the South Carolina Memorial, including the demand for suffrage, jury service, equal treatment on public conveyances and public education. In its Address the convention warned that the freedmen will not "remain dormant and disinterested, while you are making laws to govern us under such different relations as obtained in our State before we were freed." New laws were now needed, it declared, which "should either recognize our rights as a people, or else the State should not exact from us the tribute of a people, for taxation without representation is contrary to the fundamental principles which govern republican countries." [5] The freedmen were learning quickly the principles of bourgeois revolutions and quoted to good advantage one of the chief axioms of political liberty which the colonies had used against England.

Pressure was also being applied directly to President Johnson. A delegation of representative Negroes, including Frederick Douglass and George Downing (who was to play an important rôle in the labor movement), visited the President on February 7, 1866, to ask the enforcement of the Thirteenth Amendment and the granting of full rights to Negroes. The delegation represented Negro conventions and organizations of twenty states. Johnson tried to evade the issues by declaring that to give the Negroes more rights would antagonize the "poor whites" further against them. The delegation replied in a published statement:

The hostility between the whites and blacks of the South is easily explained. It has its root and sap in the relation of slavery, and was incited on both sides by the cunning of the slavemasters. Those masters secured their ascendency over both the poor whites and the blacks by putting enmity between them. They divided both to conquer each.... Slavery is abolished. The cause of the antagonism is removed.[6]

The antagonism, however, would not so easily disappear. Johnson had insinuated a course which would take advantage of this antagonism remaining from slavery, and which the Bourbons would later utilize to secure their restoration.

The Negro conventions in the South, the steps taken by the Negro masses to secure their rights and to obtain land, as well as the Equal Rights conventions held in the North at this time, clearly indicate that the Negro people were fully conscious of the issues of the new epoch. What is more, these events show that the Negroes had entered the political scene as a vital force capable of exerting independent pressure for the attainment of their demands. They were not, as so many of our historians love to depict them, an inarticulate social mass, ready to accept anything offered them, and acting as a mere ballast for the Republican ship of state in the South. On the contrary, the Negroes were an important force which had to be reckoned with by both sides. They entered upon the stage of revolution with their banners unfurled and their slogans clearly formulated. Whenever Congress had been ready to adopt a revolutionary course in Reconstruction, it would have found ready response and support among the impatient Negro masses.

Rise of the Industrial Bourgeoisie

MEANWHILE, events were leading to a rapid realignment and crystallization of class forces throughout the country. It was a period in which all classes were in state of constant flux. Released from the restraints of chattel slavery, capitalism was entering the period of its most rapid development. This economic upheaval shifted the position of all classes in relation to the fundamental social phenomenon of the period: the rise of the industrial bourgeoisie. The quick emergence of this sector from the large and shifting middle class mass, necessarily reorientated all strata of the population, creating new class antagonisms or maturing and sharpening those which had already emerged in the earlier period. The industrial bourgeoisie acted like a pole of a magnet, attracting or repelling this or that class force. The position of each class and stratum of a class can be defined and understood only in relation to the emergence of this new power.

During the war, industrialists had fattened on government contracts. A new term, "shoddy aristocracy," appeared in the language of the people to designate manufacturers who were getting rich by clothing the army. Soldiers were "picking chicken feathers out of their woolen overcoats" while New England factories declared dividends of from ten to forty percent on watered stock. The manufacture of sewing machines mounted rapidly; iron manufacturers grew wealthy on government contracts; associations of employers arose in nearly all industries. Fortunes were being rapidly accumulated. In 1863, hundreds of capitalists in New York alone had from one to twenty million dollars each, while a dry goods merchant and two railroad and land speculators (Cornelius Vanderbilt and William

Astor) were paying income taxes on from one to two million dollars annually.[7]

Industrial expansion and the extension of the factory system continued with even greater speed after the war. The output of pig iron is one of the best indicators of the growth of basic industry; between 1860 and 1870 its production had more than doubled, while the output of bituminous coal had grown two and a half times.[8] In the two decades following 1860 the number of cotton spindles had increased more than twofold. Factories were multiplying rapidly, superseding the domestic and hand mode of manufacture. In 1859 there were 140,433 establishments (factories and hand and neighborhood industries), employing 1,311,246 workers. During the next decade the number of establishments rose almost 80% to 252,148, employing 2,053,996 workers, an increase of over 56%. In the years 1870-80 the process of combination into larger manufacturing units was already introducing the era of trusts and monopolies: the number of establishments increased less than one percent while the number of workers employed in them mounted by 33 percent.[9]

The railroads were extending internal markets overnight and drawing an increasing farm population within the orbit of world commerce. Railroad mileage doubled during the Civil War decade, while Congress between 1850 and 1871 handed the railroad companies millions of acres of land (an area, according to Shannon, almost equal to Texas and Oklahoma combined).[10]

A tremendous home market was opened for American industry. During the war years the population of Illinois, Wisconsin, Minnesota and Iowa increased by almost 800,000, most of it on new lands and in the rapidly growing towns. During the same period the manufacture of mowing machines more than tripled and the output of other farm machinery grew in the same proportion. The trek westward continued at a rapid pace until, by 1880, continuous settlement stretched from coast to coast, and the United States was the most important grain exporting country.[11] The commercial farm areas became one of the most important markets for the products of industry. The war had also broadened the Southern market by creating a larger purchasing public and destroying the basis for British competition in the home market.

The industrialists were fast emerging as the dominant force in American economy and nothing could now halt their political victory. During the war they had already scored heavily in the strong protectionist tariff measure of 1864; in new financial legislation which accelerated the massing of capital in the hands of bankers; in the land grants to the railroads; in the Homestead Law of 1862 which facilitated the settlement of the West. The Immigration Act of 1864 had permitted importing workers under contract (similar to the indenture of colonial days) to be used by the capitalists to keep wages down and overcome the labor shortage created by the westward migration to the free lands and by the rapid rise of industry. In a few years this exuberant advance of the bourgeoisie was to be interrupted by the resistance of expropriated and swindled farmers and by the stormy rise of a labor movement. But meanwhile the industrial bourgeoisie reached for political power with which to protect its gains and nourish its growth.

Victory of the Left in Congress

POLITICAL power, however, could only be won and maintained by consolidating the gains of the Civil War and preventing a Southern restoration. The struggle of the industrial bourgeoisie for national power was therefore inseparable for a time from the battle for democracy in the South. The immediate needs of the bourgeoisie dictated a revolutionary course.

The first step of the parliamentary Left was to prevent the readmittance of the states "reconstructed" by President Johnson. Even before Johnson delivered his first annual message announcing the restoration of the former Confederate states, Thaddeus Stevens introduced the resolution providing for a joint committee of the House and Senate to investigate conditions in the Southern states and determine whether they were fit to return to the Union. The resolution also provided that no Congressman should be admitted from the South until the report of the Committee was made and acted upon and that all matters concerning the representation of these states should be referred to the Committee without debate. The Joint Committee on Reconstruction, consisting of 15 members with Stevens as Chairman, was thus set up to constitute an insurmountable barrier to restoration. The resolution, which was passed in February 1866, denied representation to the Southern states, without even granting them a hearing. (Many of the Congressmen chosen by the Johnson electorate had been Confederate leaders, including even Alexander H. Stephens, Vice-President of the Confederacy.) All matters pertaining to Reconstruction now had to go first before the Committee, which became, in effect, the supreme council of the revolution. Johnson's whole scheme was thus nullified at one stroke.

This was the first step towards bourgeois dictatorship in the Reconstruction of the South. The President termed the Committee "an irresponsible Central Directory, assuming nearly all the powers of Congress." It had become quite the custom on the part of the

Right to damn the Radicals in terms taken from the Great French Revolution. Even during the war days, Stevens and his adherents were already being called Jacobins to designate their resemblance to the Left group in the French Revolution. The term was used in a damning, derisive, derogatory sense. But American Jacobins they were and they should have borne the name proudly.

The Radical Republicans, now in control of Congress, overrode one Presidential veto after another, proceeding towards the Reconstruction Acts, their great *coup d'état*. Preliminaries included: The Civil Rights Bill (April 1866) which empowered the President to use the armed forces to guarantee freedmen equality before the law in matters of property and in security of person; the Freedmen's Bureau Bill (July 1866), extending the life of the Bureau another two years and, by granting it jurisdiction over freedmen and loyal refugees, constituting it as the arm of the Federal power in the South; and the Fourteenth Amendment.

The complicated device attached to the Constitution as the Fourteenth Amendment * was a compromise measure. It displays more adequately than any other legal action taken at this time the conflicting tendencies in the bourgeois democracy.

The first section of the Amendment indirectly confers citizenship upon Negroes and forbids any state to "abridge the privileges or immunities of citizens" or "deprive any person of life, liberty or property without due process of law." It recognizes clearly the rights of Negroes as citizens, but it also deliberately provides that now infamous "due process of law" clause for the protection of corporations. The meaning of this clause was not generally realized at the time the Amendment was passed. But subsequently, John A. Bingham, a Re-

* See Appendices, Document 6.

publican member of the Committee on Reconstruction and a prominent railroad lawyer, and Roscoe Conkling, also a member of the Committee and a successful corporation counsel, told how they had deliberately framed the wording of this section so that it would apply to "corporate" as well as individual persons. In a speech in Congress, Bingham enlightened his colleagues on the mysteries of the formula.

Conkling gave the more thorough explanation while arguing a tax case before the Supreme Court, where he declared that the Amendment was designed to protect "individuals and joint stock companies" who were

appealing for congressional and administrative protection against invidious and discriminating state and local taxes. ... That complaints of oppression in respect of property and other rights made by citizens of Northern States who took up residence in the South were rife in and out of Congress, none of us can forget. ... Those who devised the Fourteenth Amendment wrought in grave sincerity. They planted in the Constitution a monumental truth to stand four square to whatever wind might blow. That truth is but the golden rule, so entrenched as to curb the many who would do to the few as they would not have the few do to them.[12]

The golden rule was supplied, the Supreme Court had only to take the hint. It decided that the phrase applied to "corporate" as well as natural persons. From 1868 to 1912, the Supreme Court rendered 604 decisions based upon the Amendment, of which 312 concerned corporations. There were 28 appeals to the Court involving Negro rights under the Fourteenth Amendment, of which 22 were decided adversely.[13]

The principal political problem of Reconstruction is treated in the second section of the Amendment, this time a thoroughly deliberated compromise on the question of Negro suffrage. Under slavery, Southern representation in Congress was based on the free population plus three-fifths of the slaves. Now that there were slaves no longer and the Negro had been declared a citizen, Southern representation on the basis of its total free population would be increased. Under the three-fifths apportionment of 1860, the Southern states were entitled to 70 representatives; under the new conditions their number would be increased to eighty-three. Without granting the Negro the franchise, the former slave oligarchy, together with the Democrats of the North, could always obtain a majority in Congress and in the Electoral College. "They will at the very first election," warned Stevens, "take possession of the White House and the Halls of Congress" and even threaten the reëstablishment of slavery.

But the Radical Republicans were not yet ready to grant the universal franchise. Instead they provided in Section 2 that the basis of representation in any state shall be reduced in proportion that it denies the vote to citizens. In effect, this meant that if the former slave oligarchy chose to deny the vote to Negroes it would have to pay by reducing its representation in the House to forty-five. This is not the language of revolution. It smacks of the bickerings of narrow politicians, willing to accept a Restoration South providing it did not threaten the hegemony of the Republican bourgeoisie. Sumner denounced the compromise vigorously; Senator Julian declared: "It was a proposition to the Rebels that if they would agree that the Negroes should not be counted in the basis of representation, we would hand them over, unconditionally, to the tender mercies of their old masters." [14] But it was finally accepted by the Radicals as a concession to the Conservative Republicans.

In other sections the Amendment excludes from holding national or state office former leaders of the

Confederacy until pardoned by Congress; repudiates all debts of the Confederacy and declares the validity of the existing debts of the Federal government.

From the 1866 Congressional elections, which were waged chiefly around the issue of Reconstruction, the Radical Republicans emerged with a much stronger majority in both Houses. Johnson had encouraged every effort of the Bourbons to maintain power and his policy had borne fruit in the ferocious attacks by Bourbon mobs upon Negroes meeting in convention and fighting for their rights. Hundreds of Negroes were massacred in a series of "riots" during 1866—Memphis (May 1-3), Charleston (June 24), and the most severe at New Orleans (July 30) where the police led a Bourbon mob shooting down hundreds of Negroes and white Republicans as they were gathered in their Convention Hall. Johnson's policy was repudiated decisively in the elections and the Left was now in a better position to push a radical policy through stormy parliamentary battles, which included the impeachment of Johnson and which culminated in the Reconstruction Acts, the crowning glory of Radical Republican policy.

The Reconstruction Acts

THE Johnsonian states, on the advice of their mentor in the White House, had contemptuously rejected the Fourteenth Amendment. The Joint Committee on Reconstruction replied with its first Bill of February 1867, setting forth a comprehensive revolutionary course for Reconstruction. "There was hardly a line in the entire bill," wails Burgess, leading constitutional historian on the Civil War period, "which would stand the test of the Constitution." Neither more nor less constitutional than the Civil War itself, the Reconstruction Act * closes the Johnsonian phase of reaction and announces

* See Appendices, Document 4.

The attack upon the freedmen and Loyalists as they marched to their convention hall in New Orleans, July 30, 1866.—*Harpers Weekly*, Aug. 25, 1866.

a revolutionary cycle as grandiose as any in American history.

Sweeping into the limbo of history the civil governments established in the South by Johnson, the Act declared that in the ten * "rebel states" no legal governments or adequate protection of life and property existed. They were divided into five military districts, each under the command of a brigadier-general with sufficient forces at his disposal to enforce martial law. Under the armed dictatorship of the bourgeoisie, reconstruction was to proceed on the basis of a new democratic electorate, including the Negroes and excluding the leading Confederates. This new body of voters was to elect a Constitutional Convention which was to frame a new state Constitution embodying universal manhood suffrage. The Constitution was to be approved by a majority of the voters and by Congress. And then, only after the new state legislatures had approved the Fourteenth Amendment, and this Amendment had been ratified by the necessary number of states, were the Southern communities to be readmitted to the Union.

Three other measures passed at the same time performed the necessary operation on the powers of President Johnson. The Tenure-of-Office Bill, under which his impeachment was subsequently tried, forbade the President to remove office-holders except with the consent of the Senate. Another measure deprived the President of authority to pardon persons who had participated in the Confederate rebellion. The third forbade the President to issue military orders except through the General of the Army. Grant was General-in-Chief and was already coöperating with the Radical Republicans.

* Tennessee was not included since it ratified the Fourteenth Amendment and had been readmitted.

In addition, three supplementary Reconstruction Acts reaffirmed the principal points of the first and authorized the military commanders in the South to proceed with the reconstruction plan. It was made even clearer, due to the President's insistence upon misinterpretation of the first Act, that all leading Confederates were completely disqualified, even if they had previously received a presidential pardon.*

Two years after the end of the war, matured by its own economic development and pressed by mass upheavals in the South, the bourgeoisie embarked upon a revolutionary course. It adopted the method of armed dictatorship against reaction and assured itself a mass base in the South by disfranchising the leaders of counter-revolution and extending suffrage to the Negro. Dictatorship it was, and only philistines can deny it. But it was the kind of dictatorship which arises in every revolutionary epoch as the weapon of a new class in power, a weapon wielded against the former ruling class and against every attempt at restoration.

Looking at this dictatorship from the perspective of history one can only lament the fact that it was not dictatorial enough, that it did not immediately press forward to more decisive action against the Bourbons, such as the confiscation of their lands and property,

---

* The Second Reconstruction Act (March 23, 1867) provided detailed procedure for the reconstruction of the States. The Third Act (July 19, 1867), clearing up ambiguities in the first two, established the paramount authority of the military commanders and of Congress over the existing Johnsonian state governments and made it plain that ex-Confederate leaders were disfranchised. The Fourth Act (March 11, 1868) provided that any election be decided by the votes actually cast, altering the provision of the Second Act which required that a majority of the registered voters should accept the new state constitution before that state was readmitted. The Fourth Act was necessitated by the defeat of the Alabama constitution due to the absence from the polls of a majority of the registered voters.

their banishment or imprisonment, if necessary. Stevens' "Jacobins" could have learned many good lessons from their predecessors in the French Revolution and put them to good use in the South. But the Second American Revolution took place at a much later period, when the bourgeoisie was already so highly matured that, in relation to a rising proletariat and farming middle class in the North, it was becoming reactionary. The rapidity of capitalist development was sapping seriously the revolutionary potency of the bourgeoisie. By the time the Reconstruction Acts were passed a cynical newspaper correspondent could suggest that Congress permanently adjourn and inscribe on its doors: "The business of this establishment will be done hereafter in the office of the Pennsylvania Railroad."

Nevertheless, a new phase of the social revolution had been inaugurated in the South.

CHAPTER IV

FIGHTING FOR DEMOCRACY

The Union Leagues

WE now approach a phase of the revolution which most historians have condemned with the vilest calumny and buried under a mountain of misrepresentation. Historians who have sided with the North and historians with Bourbon sympathies essentially agree in their denunciation of so-called Black Domination and in their glee at the restoration of "home rule" in the South.

Claude Bowers in his *Tragic Era,* raves and gloats in the more violent language of an extreme reactionary. James F. Rhodes, in his eight-volume history of the period, bewails in more moderate terms the "enfranchising of ignorance and the disfranchising of intelligence." John W. Burgess considers Negro suffrage "one of the 'blunder-crimes' of the century" because it established "barbarism in power over civilization." Woodrow Wilson, who later spoke so glibly about the self-determination of peoples, can justify the Black Codes in his five-volume history and view the Reconstruction era in the South as a dark epoch of devastation wrought by Northern adventurers and "ignorant" Negroes.[1] And so *ad infinitum* runs this sickening record of American historiography. There are, of course, rare exceptions, some attempting impartiality, others indifferent, and a rare few rising to a spirited defense of the Reconstruction governments (like Dr. W. E. B. Du Bois in *Black Reconstruction*). But to offset these we have recently been deluged with dozens of volumes on the glories of the old slave South and sympathetic biographies of its leaders.

Only a profoundly revolutionary epoch can call forth such sharp denunciations even from the pens of cloistered scholars. The new history books still tremble with the violent clashes of Reconstruction. For a social revolution was initiated which today has still to be consummated.

The Reconstruction Acts had provided the legal framework within which the transformation was to take place. Military protection against the interference of the former slavemasters was provided, although it proved to be inadequate. Throughout the South at this time there were not quite 20,000 Federal troops,[2] averaging 2,000 per rebel state, and these were certainly inadequate to cope with the terrorism of reaction. They were supplemented by loyal citizens' militia and rifle clubs, composed mostly of Negroes, which in practice played a more important rôle than the troops in combating intimidation and terror.

The most important revolutionary organizations in the South were the Union (or Loyal) Leagues, organized as political centers and clubs by white and Negro Radical Republicans. Their precursors in the North were the Union League Clubs of Philadelphia, New York, and Boston which were formed after the first year of war. Similar Leagues soon appeared in all parts of the North. They represented the militantly patriotic and radical wing of the bourgeoisie, mobilizing support and supplies for the Northern troops, enlisting Negroes, caring for freedmen in camps in the North and carrying on an agitational campaign among the former slaves and poorer whites in the conquered territories. The Clubs became a center of opposition to the Johnson-Bourbon alliance and agitated energetically for Radical

Reconstruction. The Leagues, especially in the East, were largely dominated by industrialists and bankers, including the financier and stockbroker Jay Cooke who was later to figure in the large-scale financing of railroads and the panic of 1873. The distribution of four and a half million agitational pamphlets between 1865 and 1868 by the Philadelphia League alone indicates the extensive activities of the organization.

As early as 1863 the Leagues took root in the South among the white classes opposing the slavocracy, and spread as the Union Army occupied Southern territory. In a few months after the close of the war the organization extended throughout the upland white counties in the South. Its membership included the so-called Loyalists in the states of the lower South, the Union elements in the border states, Army officers and officials of the Freedmen's Bureau. Probably one-third of the white population of the upland districts in 1866 was in the Leagues.[3] These played an important rôle in organizing the first anti-Bourbon state governments at the close of the war in Kentucky and Tennessee and in all likelihood directed what opposition there was in the Johnson Restoration governments of the other states.

The Leagues also appeared early in the very heart of the plantation area. Chief Justice Chase, while on a visit to a number of Southern states, wrote President Johnson on May 21, 1865, that "everywhere throughout the country colored citizens are organizing Union Leagues." He sensed that they "must exert a great influence on the future of the class they represent, and not a little bit on the character of the states in which they exist" and advised Johnson that they constituted "a power which no wise statesman will despise." [4] The Chief Justice proved to be correct.

While the Leagues in the North were becoming selective social clubs, in the South they developed as the organizational centers of the popular movement, in some respects similar to the Jacobin Clubs of the French Revolution. They became units of a well disciplined organization and by 1867 played a decisive rôle in preparing for the new Constitutional Conventions. All the Negro leaders were members, and branches existed in every Negro community. The local Council of the League in each election district met weekly. A State Council, with headquarters in the capital city, united the local bodies through an executive committee consisting of two representatives from each county. There was a National Grand Council in New York. Women were organized in auxiliaries of the local Councils. "But for the strong organization and iron discipline of the order," stated a contemporary, "the blacks would have been unable to vote ... and thus the purposes of Reconstruction would have been defeated." [5]

During the preliminary period of organization of mass support for the revolutionary state governments, the Leagues proved indispensable. They were the heart of the revolution. The constant raids by Bourbon guerrilla bands on the Councils show where the pivotal organizational strength of the popular revolution reposed. The Negroes often transformed the Councils into people's militia companies and rifle clubs for purposes of self-defense. While the Leagues included white Radical Republicans from the North (derisively termed "carpetbaggers" by the reactionaries), native white Republicans (even more derisively termed "scalawags") and military officers, most of its members were Negroes. The Negro looked upon this organization as his own. "He will stop from work 'in the middle of a row' to attend its meetings," wrote a Bourbon. "He will slink away from his employer, after all protestations to the contrary to vote the Radical ticket, at the secret command of this new political society." In Virginia, continues the same writer, everyone was surprised "at the solid array in which the Negroes moved to the polls in the vote for the Convention." Over 800 Councils existed in the State.[6]

According to another account, the emblems of the Union Leagues included the Altar and the Holy Bible, the Declaration of Independence and the Union Flag, the sword and the ballot box, the sickle and the anvil, and other emblems of industry. In some places the Councils were known as "Red Strings," "Heroes of America," "Grant Rangers," "National Guards." Though available records are unreliable as to details because of their counter-revolutionary bias, it is nevertheless evident that the Leagues were basically mass organizations, the real "storm centers" of the revolution.

One observer described their activities as follows:

The meetings of the Councils were held once a week in Negro churches and schoolhouses, around which armed guards were stationed; inflammatory speeches were made by carpetbaggers and Negro leaders; confiscation and division of property and social rights were promised.... The members went armed to the meetings and were there trained in military drill, often after dark, much to the alarm of the whites in the community. In South Carolina the Loyal Leagues were simply the Negro militia. Military parades were frequently held. If a white person became obnoxious to the League, his buildings were likely to be burned.[7]

Without the Councils and militias, wholesale massacres would have resulted every time the Negroes attempted to vote or otherwise participate in political life. In many places they would mete out direct punishment to their persecutors. In South Carolina, for example, the Leaguers assembled 300 strong around the house of a white man who had wounded a Negro and would have dealt with him in their own way, had not a detachment of troops intervened.[8] The records are full of accounts of stubborn and armed resistance by the Negroes against all efforts to deprive them of the rights they had won. Morgan, a Radical Republican farmer and "carpetbagger" in Yazoo City, Miss., the very heart of the Black Belt, tells in a book entitled *Yazoo, or on the Picket Line of Freedom in the South,* how carefully and militantly the Negro plantation workers guarded his life against Bourbon attacks. On more than one occasion they saved him from lynching; when planters tried to take Morgan's life at the Mississippi Constitutional Convention, his Negro friends protected him; armed with hickory sticks and a few pistols they escorted him to the Sunday School every week.[9]

Throughout this period a constant struggle was waged, on the plantations, in the towns, at the polling places, at the crossroads. Each step meant struggle. Every time the Negro voted he had to fight for the right. One observer tells how in Mississippi the Negroes marched to the polls "after the manner of soldiers, armed with clubs and sticks, some of them with old swords and pieces of scythe blades." [10] With arms the freedman was forced to defend his schoolhouses and his churches.

The Republican Party

WITH the Union Leagues as a basis, the Republican Party formed its Southern state organizations in 1867-1868. Eleven Negroes and two whites initiated the formation of a Union Republican Party in South Carolina and presented the platform at a large mass meeting in Charleston in March 1867. The demand for "the abolition of the large estates" found a prominent place in the platform, along with universal education, protection of Negro suffrage and the other democratic demands of the period. At its inaugural convention in July, consisting of 70 delegates from 19 counties, the leaders were Northerners of both races and "a native white man of wealth." R. H. Gleaves, a mulatto, was chairman and one delegate took up the proposal of Wendell Phillips that a Negro be made Republican Vice-Presidential candidate in the next election.[11]

At the first Republican convention of Mississippi, one-third of the delegates were freedmen. They endorsed the principles of the national Party and declared in their platform that they would "keep step with it in all the progressive political reforms of the age."[12] The Virginia State convention * reiterated the democratic demands of the epoch and appealed to the "laboring classes of the State" for support, telling them that they "do not desire to deprive the laboring white men of any rights or privileges which they now enjoy, but do propose to extend these rights and privileges by the organization of the Republican Party in this State."[13]

Generally the state parties, despite an occasional emphasis upon confiscation, did not go beyond the platform of the national organization and exhibited the same contradictions as the Party in the North. While the Grand Council of the Union League of Alabama threatened in April 1867 "stiff-necked and rebellious people" with confiscation of their lands,[14] next January the Republican Party State Executive Committee, in an "Address to the Laboring Men" advised the plantation workers "to go to work and make contracts at once."[15] The Convention of the Charleston Republicans declared that "large land monopolies tend only to make the rich richer and the poor poorer and

* See Appendices, Document 3.

are ruinous to the agricultural, commercial, and social interests of the State," yet went no further on the land question than to urge division and sale of the unoccupied lands to "the poorer classes." [16] The Republican Party did not reach beyond the purely political phases of Reconstruction, and offered no other solution of the land situation than to urge a more progressive form of labor on the plantations and the splitting up of the estates by sale.

The freedmen raised the land question again and again at the Republican meetings. At political rallies in Florida, for example, the plantation Negroes often became "impudent" and announced a "Wendell Phillips' doctrine, which was that the property of the one-time masters really belonged to the one-time slaves." A former slaveowner spoke at one of these meetings in an effort to break the freedmen away from the Republicans:

We know what you are talking and doing. You are drilling over the country.... What rights do you want? The property of the whites? You intend to fight for it, do you? ... Whenever you get ready strike the blow, and you will see the hell of ruin which your radical teachers have brought you.[17]

The Negro Militias

THERE was still a third type of organization, some of whose activities we have already described in discussing the movement for land, which assumed increasing importance as Reconstruction proceeded. These were the Negro militias and rifle companies which existed throughout the South. They were formed around the core of demobilized Negro soldiers and might be described as a Citizen's Army, at first supplying themselves with whatever weapons they could obtain and later, under the Reconstruction governments, receiving aid from, and in some cases being authorized by, the state. The line of demarcation between them and the Union Leagues is often not clear. When the Leagues armed themselves and drilled they were designated as militias. When K.K.K. violence in South Carolina disrupted the original Councils of the Union League in 1870-71, their place was said to be taken by the Negro militias,[18] but this might have been simply the process of the Leagues arming and transforming themselves into military companies. They were sometimes referred to as "nigger K.K.K.s" by the local Bourbon press, and have appeared under a variety of names such as National Guards, "Whangs," the "Wide-Awakers," and in some places were named after individuals, such as the Elliott Guards and Neagle Rifles in Columbia, S. C.

Armed civilian Negroes, as we have already noted in a previous chapter, appeared upon the scene early in the revolution. It seems that these were not permanent bodies at that time. The freedmen armed themselves wherever possible, but regularly constituted regiments of the Federal Army as a rule seem to have been the only formal bodies. But beginning in 1867, about the time the Union Leagues began to play the central political rôle, civilian military companies also were formed, which engaged in drill and were regularly officered. The Macon (Ga.) *Journal and Messenger*, for example, described such companies in and around the city, which drilled regularly and comprised officers and privates, all armed.[19] The *Alabama Beacon* reported that two companies of Negroes were drilling at Brewersville in readiness for expected Ku-Klux raids.[20] At New Orleans, the Warmouth Guards organized and paraded.[21] The Governor of North Carolina was asked to disband the company of Negro militia in Wake County.[22] In Virginia the Bourbon press protested vigorously against the nightly drilling and marching of armed Negroes in the principal cities "on almost every local or national holiday." [23]

These Negro citizens' battalions were already formed, it should be noted, before the new Reconstruction state governments existed, and they appeared entirely on the initiative of the freedmen or of Negro troops. A name such as "Wide-Awakers" indicates their purpose as volunteer defense corps.

The attitude of the military governors and generals in charge of the territorial districts differed. In Florida, for example, Federal officers in 1867 forbade Negroes to attend night meetings under arms as they had been doing in a dozen counties.[24] On the other hand, General Swayne sharply rebuked a subordinate who issued an order to seize arms in the hands of freedmen in Russell County, in the heart of the plantation Black Belt of Alabama. In his reprimand, the General stated:

The Constitution of the United States commands that the right of the people to keep and bear arms, shall not be infringed, and that the right of the people to be protected in their persons, houses, papers and effects against unreasonable searches and seizures, shall not be violated.

The General warned his officer that he would support this decision with force and hold him to "a stern accountability if he should disregard it." The arming of the Negroes was clearly a class measure, as the newspaper, from which we take the account of this incident, hastened to point out. "Can the white citizens of Alabama," it asked, " 'keep and bear arms' under the Constitution of the United States, in General Swayne's opinion?" The journal answered by declaring that every day or so some white man is fined $25 by the Provost Marshal for carrying concealed weapons.[25] In the Black Belt counties, where such incidents occurred, the whites were practically all plantation owners or their hangers-on and in all likelihood were also members of the K.K.K. or similar organizations.

After 1868, under the Reconstruction governments in a number of states, the militias were authorized by the Governor and new bodies created. According to testimony before the Congressional Committee investigating the K.K.K. outrages in the South in 1870-71, numerous Negro militia companies were authorized and armed by the Governor of South Carolina on the eve of the elections of 1870, and a still later investigation placed the number in the State at 14 regiments of 1,000 men each. The opponents of the Radical Republican government charged that the arming of the Negro militias was a political move in preparation for the elections. This charge was repeated again and again in the testimony before an investigation into fraud in South Carolina after the restoration of reactionary government,[26] with the intention of showing unnecessary expenditures. Simkins and Woody in their history of Reconstruction in that State also declare that the purpose of the state-authorized militias was "to keep the Negroes in line for the coming elections." But in contradiction to this interpretation, the same authors report that the militia was most active in the up-country. "In the middle and lower counties," they say, "where the Radical majority was more certain, there seemed to be less racial antagonism. But in some up-country counties the whites had majorities, and there was a possibility that the border counties would be lost to the Radicals." [27] It should seem more likely that if the militias were so active principally in the up-country it was to protect the Negro minorities there against Bourbon aggression, and that their services were less needed in the Black Belt counties where the Negroes were well able to keep not only themselves "in line" but their enemies as well.

But there is no need to deny that the organization of the Negro militias was frankly a political move. This was the only fashion in which the Negroes could be protected in their right to vote and against victimization by K.K.K. bands. The Radical Republican governments were entirely too apologetic about taking steps such as this and retreated shamefully before the hypocritical charges of the Bourbon Democrats who themselves surreptitiously organized and armed the K.K.K. for their own political purposes.

Registration of the New Electorate

REGISTRATION of voters took place in September 1867. This was the first major political act of the revolutionary dictatorship in the South. Both sides prepared strenuously. The Reconstruction Acts provided that no conventions should be held unless the majority of the registered electorate voted on the question. The Bourbons were divided on the tactics to pursue. In some sections they counseled a boycott of the elections, hoping to prevent the necessary majority participation in the Convention vote. Another wing agreed that all whites should register, but some urged that the whites obstruct the course of Reconstruction by voting down the Convention, and others that the Reconstruction machinery be utilized to elect a Convention with Bourbon sympathies. At the same time, efforts were made everywhere to prevent registration of Negroes by violence and by threatening to discharge plantation workers who registered and voted for the Convention. Rumors were spread by the planters that registration was for the purpose of taxation or recruitment into the army. In other cases freedmen were urged to register and vote against the Convention on the ground that to defeat a Convention was to secure confiscation of the property of the rich. The *Daily State Sentinel,* Alabama Republican paper, rose to the occasion with a warning to "Union friends" that it was useless to "entertain such notions." [28]

The Union Leagues carried on tireless activity to counter intimidation and to mobilize the Negro masses for their first political move. During the spring and summer months the *Sentinel* reported numerous political rallies, parades and demonstrations throughout the plantation area. At Talladega, 2,000 Negroes paraded through the main street and joined the whites at a mass meeting in the court house where resolutions supporting the Republican Party and demanding a thorough system of common schools were passed. At Wetumka, the reporter noticed that "the more radical the speeches, the better the colored people liked them," and that the Union Leagues were "spreading like smallpox." At Uniontown, there was the same proportion of white and Negro at the mass meeting as there were white and Negro voters in the county. At all the meetings, the efforts of the Bourbons to form a "white man's party" were deprecated and the white laboring people were called upon to coöperate with the Negroes in the Republican organizations.

The Negro people defined their own position clearly. The Colored Convention of Alabama, meeting in Mobile in May 1867, issued an Address * to the people of the State, in which it explained that "it was thought best that a convention, composed entirely of our own people, should be held, before deciding upon our future political course." In the Address, the course decided upon is clearly set forth. First, it recapitulates the democratic rights thus far won, declaring that the

* See Appendices, Document 5.

Negroes claim "exactly the same rights, privileges and immunities as are enjoyed by white men." The Bourbons are notified that "we know our rights; and knowing dare to maintain them" and that if they "execute their threats of making us vote as they say or starve, we will call upon the Republican Party to deprive them of the property earned by the sweat of our brow, which they have proved themselves so unworthy to possess."

While some people preach patience and would have them wait a few months, years or generations until the Conservative whites voluntarily give them their rights, the Negro people "do not intend to wait one day longer than we are absolutely compelled to." Listing all the discriminations and wrongs which the Negroes have suffered, the Address points out that the political reorganization of the State will be largely in the hands of colored people and that if their "white friends" persist in their old course their conduct will be remembered when "we have power."

Of unusual interest is that portion of the Address which states the attitude of the Negro convention to the Republican Party. The Negro people, it says, have arrayed themselves with the Republican Party because that Party opposed the extension of slavery, repealed the fugitive slave law, abolished slavery, put down the Confederate rebellion, passed the Freedmen's Bureau and Civil Rights Bills, enfranchised the colored people, provided for a political reorganization of the South, and passed the Homestead Bill, in short, "it is the only party which has ever attempted to extend our privileges." It is true, the Address recognizes, that some Republicans care nothing for the principles of the Party, "but it is also certainly true that ninety-nine-hundredths of all those who were conscientiously in favor of our rights were and are in the Republican

Party, and that the great mass of those who hated, slandered and abused us were and are in the opposition party."

There certainly could have been no better reasons for the Negroes to support the Republican Party at that time. The reasons are precisely and clearly enumerated in this document, and set forth as the fully conscious position of the Negro people. But the Address goes even further in presenting an independent position. With prophetic vision, the Republicans are warned that the main strategy of their opponents will be to divide them along race lines. It is urged that "the most effectual method of preserving our unity will be for us to always act together—never to hold separate political meetings or caucuses." In nominations for office, the Address warns, the Negro people expect that there will be no discrimination on account of color and while they realize that there are not enough sufficiently trained Negroes to fill the higher offices, when qualified men are found they must not be rejected because of being black. Finally, every member of the Republican Party is earnestly called upon to demand the establishment of universal public education so that "our children when they come upon the stage of action" will not suffer from the handicaps imposed by slavery.[29]

With such clear definitions of the issues at stake and of their own political position, the Negro people pursued their battle for democracy. It was a difficult struggle which had to contend with obstacles of all sorts. But the people were in motion. Their temper was expressed by Lewis Lindsay, a Negro worker of Virginia, who replied to the employers' threat of economic boycott that "before any of his children would suffer for food, the streets of Richmond should run knee-deep in blood; and he thanked God that the

Negroes had learned to use guns, pistols and ram-rods."

The registration of voters was the first legal sanction of the revolution to Negro suffrage. The large Negro registration was a tribute to the effectiveness of their organizations, for their political opponents were their employers, and to register meant to overcome obstinate resistance and trickery at their very door-steps. Registration produced a new electorate of over 700,000 Negroes and 660,000 whites in the ten rebel states. The Negro registration alone almost equalled the total vote in these states (720,000) in the elections of 1860. The number of former Confederates disqualified is estimated at about 200,000. Thus was democracy in the South for the first time extended to the Negroes and also to new sections of the white population. "The highest social class," mourns Rhodes, "the men of brains, character and experience—were disfranchised while the lowest of the low were given a vote." [30]

The Political Geography of the South and the Rôle of the Whites

THE registration of voters revealed the class and racial geography of the revolution in the South. The Negroes registered large majorities in South Carolina, Mississippi, Louisiana and Alabama; a majority in the small number of Florida electors; almost half of the registered electorate in Georgia; while in Virginia, North Carolina, Arkansas and Texas the white voters were in the majority. Allowing for the disfranchising of the active Confederates, white and Negro voters were registered in about the same proportion as their ratio in the population of the various states. In South Carolina the Negroes comprised about 60% of the population and 63% of the registered voters; in Mississippi

55% of the population and the majority of the registered electorate (no figures by color were reported); in Louisiana 50% of the population and 65% of the voters; and in Alabama 45% of the population and 63% of the voters (in the almost purely white northern section of the State, registration was not vigorously pushed); in Georgia 44% of the population and 49% of the electorate.

The revolution attained its highest level in those states where the plantation Black Belts played by far the dominant economic and political rôle, as in South Carolina, Mississippi and Louisiana. The plantation area, where the Negroes constituted the overwhelming majority of the population, extends in irregular crescent shape from southeastern Virginia, forms a narrow neck through North Carolina, engulfs practically all of South Carolina with the exception of a small up-land section in the northwest, cuts diagonally across the center of Georgia separating the northern and southern white areas of the State, forms a wide swathe across the southern half of Alabama, expands into a broad horizontal shape along the Mississippi River from Memphis to New Orleans and reaches into eastern Texas.[31] Outside of this area there were relatively few Negroes and in the Black Belt color was pretty strictly the designation of class. The Negroes were the plantation workers; the whites were the plantation owners, overseers, bosses and civil authorities of the slave oligarchy, with a very slight sprinkling of white derelicts of the system, either entirely landless or owners of a few cast-off acres.

This economic and class situation finds its clearest political expression during Reconstruction in the three states we have mentioned because here state politics most clearly and directly reflected the struggle between the two principal contending social forces: the Negro peasantry and the large planters. These were almost entirely agrarian areas. The portions of these states which were not in the Black Belt played an inconsequential rôle in the economy of the state, being inhabited largely by small peasant farmers in a domestic economy.

In the other states, however, there existed a more equal division between the plantation Black Belt and the white yeoman up-lands, as in Alabama. In still others, such as Georgia and North Carolina, there was in addition a higher level of industrial development and a more matured urban middle class. Reconstruction, therefore, proceeded irregularly in various portions of the South depending upon the peculiarities of sectional and class developments in each state.

Nevertheless, it is possible to make some generalities about the rôle of the white population in the South at this time. In the first place, it is necessary to dissipate the usual assumption that the whites constitued one whole undifferentiated mass arrayed against the Negro. The real slave oligarchy, if we count among its members those holding more than 20 slaves, comprised only three percent of the white population of the slave states. They held the reins of state power under slavery, dominating the economy and political life of the South. Non-slaveholders, generally and erroneously bunched together under the term "poor whites," constituted more than three-fourths of the white population of the slave states. Of these barely 100,000 were town artisans and mechanics or workers in the few factories, only some of whom could be called proletarians in the real meaning of the term. Most of the others were agrarians of various economic and social strata.

Mountaineers of the Appalachians were self-sufficing peasant farmers and hunters, producing entirely for their own needs and cut off from all markets. They were not really drawn into modern life on any large scale until the development of the textile industry in the South after 1880, when many of them were forced off the land by mining and lumber companies and migrated to the mill villages. But during Reconstruction they were never drawn on any important scale into the popular revolution and played an inconsequential rôle in the politics of the era.

The largest sector of the non-slaveholding white population was the white yeomanry which played an important, and often, decisive rôle in Reconstruction politics. The small farmers were most numerous outside the cotton and plantation belt and were dominant in the Piedmont along the northern fringe of the Black Belt (Virginia, North Carolina, northwest corner of South Carolina, northern Georgia and Alabama) and some portions of eastern Mississippi. Most of the small farmers also lived largely on a domestic basis, producing for the market only occasionally. Under the slave system they supplied only 15% of the cotton crop.

A third section consisting of the so-called "crackers," "clay-eaters," etc., might be described as the *lumpen*-proletarians of the slave system, scattered along the fringes of the plantation regions and in the pine barrens, living largely on occasional crumbs thrown them by the planters, who recruited from their ranks plantation bosses and guards. They were not entirely landless; many of them cultivated a few acres and raised occasional livestock, but they were generally speaking unimportant to the economic life of the region. They were probably not as numerous as is generally supposed.[32]

During slavery, the small farmers had offered the principal resistance to the oligarchy and during the war large sections of the up-lands remained loyal to

the Union. Rowan Helper's *The Impending Crisis,*
written on the eve of the Civil War, although display-
ing deep prejudice against the Negro, bears eloquent
testimony to the small farmers' opposition to slavery
and the oligarchy. The defeat of the slavemasters in
war and the revolutionary changes in the South extended democracy to broader sections of the whites.
It was now possible to reform a system in which the
"Laws were made by the owners of plantations; governors of states were of their choosing and members of
Congress were selected and maintained in accordance
with their wishes." [33]

In the Johnsonian state governments of 1865-66, the
up-country representatives opposed the planters and
exerted a democratic influence. At the South Carolina Constitutional Convention of 1865, for example,
the up-land delegates forced the abolition of the parish
system which had always guaranteed the plantation
owners of the Black Belt dominant representation in
the state government, and forced other reforms such
as abolishing property qualifications for legislators and
a more uniform system of taxation. They were, however, opposed to Negro suffrage out of fear that the
planters would be able to maintain domination through
control of the Negro votes in the Black Belt.[34] In
many of the constitutional conventions held under the
Johnson restoration the white farmers' representatives
pressed for the repudiation of the Confederate debts as
demanded by Congress.

The revolution also removed the chief obstacle to
the economic development of the small farmers. Due
to general economic chaos and crop failures in the
years immediately after the war, large planters were
unable to meet their obligations and their land was
thrown upon the auction block. Land values dropped
drastically; plantations that had brought $100,000 and

$150,000 before the war, were sold at $6,000 or $10,000. To a certain degree the larger plantations were cut up and sold in smaller parcels and the small white farmer bought up land in the richer plantation regions.[35] The abolition of slavery also made possible a freer agrarian development, the extension of town and city markets and greater participation in world commerce. Although it would take time for these economic aspects of the revolution to make themselves fully felt, the yeomen farmers were already reacting to their influence.

The mass of the small farming whites was therefore in a different economic category than the Negroes. These whites as a class were evolving from a self-sufficing peasant economy in the direction of middle class capitalist farmers, while the Negroes emerged from chattel slavery without land to become a class of agrarian toilers whose economic status stood midway between chattel slavery and free wage-labor or plantation tenancy. A real economic class distinction between the agrarian whites and Negroes existed, which tended to prolong the sharp prejudices established by chattel slavery. Nevertheless, the white middle and small farmers were decidedly opposed to the reëstablishment of political power based upon the large landed estates. On these grounds, they might throw their support as allies to the bourgeois revolution.

But other forces tended to push them in the opposite direction. They were also in that position which had been so graphically described by President Johnson: threatened on the one hand by the domination of the big planters and on the other by the oligarchy of big capitalists. While much of the legislation of the new Reconstruction state legislatures would favor the small farmers, the tariff and financial and railroad policies of the national government tended to alienate them. But this in itself was not sufficient to turn them against the bourgeois democracy and make them follow the old-line Southern leadership.

Would they ally themselves with the Negroes, the most reliable mass support of the bourgeois democratic dictatorship in the South? Would the antagonism between them and the planters be sufficiently sharp to overcome the pernicious prejudices created by the chattel slave system? Would they ally themselves with a people whom they had been taught to look upon as an inferior race which had been subjected and oppressed by "their own" white nation? In the situation which prevailed on the eve of the establishment of the new governments such an alliance could have been facilitated and assured if more drastic action were taken against the leaders of the old régime. Confiscation of their property and the creation of a Negro yeomanry would have established the economic basis for such coöperation. And the voice of counter-revolution should have been more effectively stilled. Leading Bourbons were disfranchised, but they were permitted the fullest freedom of agitation and propaganda. They could appeal to the prejudices of the slave system and seek restoration under the battle cry of defending "white civilization" against "black barbarism."

The vote for the Constitutional Conventions was the first indication of what course the agrarian middle class would pursue. Some of the old leaders had told them to vote for the holding of the Conventions and elect Democrats and Conservatives as delegates, while others had called upon them to obstruct Reconstruction by voting down the call for a Convention or by boycotting the elections entirely. The Radical Republicans had appealed to them to form a common front with the Negroes against the Bourbon Democrats. The results of the plebiscite do not supply a decisive answer on this point. In the seven states in which separate figures for the white voters were reported * 107,999 whites voted for the Convention, 116,896 against it, and 278,064 registered white voters abstained. The only categorical stand was taken by those who voted against holding the Convention. The Bourbon reaction could as yet count definitely only upon this group, comprising less than one-fourth of the registered white electorate.

The white group which voted for the Convention, numerically almost equal to the anti-Conventionists, could not generally be relied upon to give unstinted support to the revolutionary democracy. Undoubtedly it included a strong pro-Radical sector, but it also included those who had voted for the Convention and elected delegates who would pursue a conciliatory, if not outright reactionary course. The Georgia plebiscite was indicative of its prevailing attitude. Joseph E. Brown, former governor of the State under the slavocracy, urged compliance with the Reconstruction Acts under which the Democratic Party should work for the control of the South. He was bitterly opposed by Benjamin H. Hill, extreme Bourbon politician, who urged voting against the Convention. The Georgia white vote stood: 32,000 for, 4,000 against, 60,000 abstaining. The white up-lands voted for the Convention and reflected a strong anti-Bourbon sentiment but, as subsequent developments showed, this section did not prove to be a reliable ally of the Black Belt democracy.

The abstention of more than half the registered white voters in the seven states also cannot be interpreted as indicating a definite political stand. Undoubtedly many of the country poor were intimidated

* The results are not given by color of voter in Mississippi, Arkansas and Louisiana.

by the planters and did not participate in the plebiscite for this reason. On the other hand, the large abstention cannot be interpreted entirely as a victory for the Bourbon obstructionist policy. Even the most extreme opponents of radical Reconstruction, such as Hill of Georgia, counseled voting against the Convention, but nevertheless, voting. The extreme reactionaries were defeated and the action of the majority of white voters in abstaining indicated at most that while they were opposed to revolutionary political measures they preferred to wait and see. As far as it is possible to generalize about the attitude of the white voters it can be said that they were an uncertain and wavering political factor, open to persuasion from either side and could be won by either side by decisive action. If not entirely won by the Radical Republicans, they might at least be neutralized.

The Negroes voted *en masse* for the Convention. Their mass support rendered possible the political revolution in the South. Events had placed in their hands the key to the door of historical progress, when history had hardly given them an opportunity to develop the necessary class leadership and political experience for the tremendous tasks which faced them. Nor had history taken the trouble to evolve in time allies upon which they could rely.

But the ex-slaves, the despised, the "lowest of the low," this "enfranchised barbarism," stepped forth upon the stage of history as the exponents and bearers of the most advanced social and political tendencies of the epoch. They were fighters fully conscious of their aims and their demands. Those specialists who have failed to grasp the grandeur of this popular revolution and have dismissed it with some generalizations about the use of the Negro vote by corrupt politicians, are not worthy of the name of historians. Having accepted as an axiom the inferiority of the Negro, they cannot possibly conceive in their philistine smugness that the Negro masses and their leaders could possibly act in the most modern civilized manner, while the civilized bearers of the slave culture were the instruments of retrogression and reaction. During revolutionary epochs finesse and culture—in the nice, polite meaning of the terms—are the attributes of the reactionary class, while the class which had been deprived of the opportunity of developing culture tends to be rough and rugged. And it was with this healthy ruggedness, from which most historians turn with dismay, that the landless tillers of the soil left their unmistakable impress upon the course of revolution in the South.

But how can a historian, even if he has an animal prejudice against Negroes, be so blind as not to see that the Negro masses constituted an independent ally of the bourgeoisie and not a mute following? Is not the very incorporation by the Republican Party in its Reconstruction program of such drastic steps for Negro liberty evidence that these demands were being persistently pushed forward by the Negro people themselves? Is it not clear that while the bourgeoisie was already finding less and less use for democratic practices in the North, they had to encourage these very practices in the South in order to retain the Negroes as allies? That the very act of the Republican Party in raising democratic revolutionary slogans had the effect of stimulating the Negro masses and of catapulting them into the struggle for their attainment? That accepting these slogans as an expression of their own needs, the Negro masses would demand a full accounting? That if extraordinary means had to be used to assure the Negro the vote and participation in government, it was not because the Negro was unwilling but that sharp reactionary resistance had to be overcome?

CHAPTER V

THE PEOPLE'S ASSEMBLIES

The Constitutional Conventions

"No such hideous bodies of men had ever been assembled before upon the soil of the United States for the purpose of participation in the creation of a State of the Union," exclaims Burgess, describing the new Constitutional Conventions.[1] "Never more astonishing conventions, in personnel, in a civilized country," agrees Claude G. Bowers, a present-day historian, in his *Tragic Era*.[2] A "Tragic Era" indeed for those who have cause to fear that history will next time speak in a more decisive voice.

The Constitutional Conventions elected by the new voters were the first really representative bodies of the people to meet on Southern soil. They were also the first state assemblies in which Negroes participated as elected representatives of the people. In the South Carolina Convention there were 48 white delegates and 76 Negro, fully two-thirds of whom had once been slaves, while the white up-country was represented by some substantial farmers and "low-down whites."[3] In Louisiana 49 delegates of each race participated. The "Black and Tan" Convention of Mississippi had 17 Negro delegates out of a total of 100, although there were 70 delegates from the 32 Black Belt counties. Negro delegates were also elected to the other constitutional conventions. But only in South Carolina and Louisiana did the Negroes participate in proportion to their ratio in the population or in the electorate.*

Most of the conventions were predominantly agrarian and directly representative of the poorer sections of the population, especially in South Carolina. The white delegates of the state paid altogether $761 in annual taxes, of which one conservative paid $508. The taxes paid by the Negro delegates totaled $117, of which a Charleston Negro paid $85. Fifty-nine of the Negro and 23 of the white delegates paid no taxes whatever. These certainly were not men of property gathered in South Carolina to create a new democratic state. Almost half of them had toiled on the plantations as slaves, others had scratched out a bare living in the up-lands.

Fully half of the 98 delegates at the Alabama convention were agrarians; 16 of the 18 Negroes had been slaves. But there was also good representation from the urban middle class: 16 lawyers, 9 physicians, 4 of other middle-class occupations, and 4 white-collar employees. Six town workers were also delegates. Contrary to the general impression created by highly prejudiced accounts that the Reconstruction bodies consisted largely of "carpetbaggers," at least 70 of the delegates were native Southerners.[4] Likewise in Mississippi, where Negroes had evidently been discriminated against in the selection of delegates,—the so-called carpetbaggers only had some 20-odd representatives, nearly all of whom had been soldiers in the Union Army and who had been elected from the Black Belt counties. On the other hand, there were 29 native white Republicans. Of the 17 Negro delegates, at least seven were ministers.[5] The Negroes had supplied the

---

* In the other states: Florida, 27 white and 18 Negro; Virginia, 80 white and 25 Negro; Georgia, 137 white and 33 Negro; Alabama, 90 white and 18 Negro; Arkansas, 58 white and 8 Negro; North Carolina, 118 white and 15 Negro; Texas, 81 white and 9 Negro.

necessary majority for calling the Convention, while it was dominated by the white delegates. In Louisiana, many of the Negro delegates were propertied free Negroes under slavery, while a good proportion once tilled the soil as slaves.

These people's conventions, the overwhelming majority of whose delegates were newly awakened peasants, proceeded to write state constitutions which would revolutionize the South if put into effect today. "These documents," rages Bowers, "framed by ignorance, malevolence, and partisanship, sounded the death-knell of civilization in the South." They did, indeed, place the official seal upon the death certificate of the slave civilization and swept aside, at least in words, all the cobwebs of history which had gathered in the corners of the oligarchy.

The new constitutions provided for Negro suffrage and for complete equality of civil rights. They disfranchised and barred from office the leaders of the Confederacy, as already stipulated in the Fourteenth Amendment. The most drastic steps in this regard were taken by Alabama, Arkansas, Mississippi and Louisiana, only the last of which had a large enough number of Negro delegates at the convention to make their action decisive. The Alabama and Arkansas constitutions disfranchised all who "had violated the rules of civilized warfare"; Louisiana disfranchised all who had voted for secession or had advocated treason against the United States. Mississippi and Virginia disbarred from office any one who had voluntarily participated in the rebellion or had voluntarily given aid. The opposition of the up-lands to the old planter aristocracy is indicated by the fact that disfranchisement was most stringent in those states where the white delegates sat as a majority in the conventions.

Other measures passed by the conventions reflect

the thoroughgoing nature of the democratic overturn. The South Carolina constitution provided that no person be disqualified for crimes committed as a slave. Property qualifications for office were abolished and representation in the Lower House was to be apportioned by population and not property, as had been the case under slavery. No one could be imprisoned for debt nor prevented from enjoying property rights. A system of universal public education was to be created. Rights of women were extended. The system of county government was reorganized, providing for the election of all county officials and enlarging county self-government. In Mississippi and Louisiana additional provisions were included to assure equal rights on all public conveyances. The University of Louisiana was opened to Negroes. Other state conventions passed similar constitutions, which embodied a complete transformation of the old social structure.

The conventions also struck at ideological remnants of the slave system. One resolution passed by the South Carolina body demanded that steps be taken to "expunge forever from the vocabulary of South Carolina, the epithets, 'nigger,' 'negro,' and 'Yankee' ... and to punish this insult by fine and imprisonment." [6] A resolution in the Mississippi body changed the name of Davis County to Jones, to extinguish any official recognition of the former president of the Confederacy.

The proceedings of the conventions show their deep roots in the soil. In Mississippi, General Gillem cooperated with the big planters and refused to permit the execution of a number of resolutions passed by the Convention. One of these would have levied a high poll tax for the relief of destitute Negroes but the General held that there was plenty of work for the freedmen if they would only go back to the plantations and not wait for the convention to pass a law giving them the land. He also objected to other resolutions requesting tax collectors to suspend collection of all taxes assessed against freedmen before January 1, 1868, and providing for the abolition of all debts, contracts and judgments that had been made early in 1865. These demands were aimed at the system of contract labor and peonage on the plantations. Still another request that all property taken from the freedmen by their former owners be returned was vetoed by the commanding General.[7]

The land question was the most frequently discussed in the South Carolina Convention. A Southern historian informs us that "some of the reforms proposed by the colored delegates" were "born of ignorant self-assertiveness; for example, the suggestion that landlords be required to pay wages from January 1, 1863," the day of Emancipation.[8] A similar resolution had been passed in the Alabama Convention.

Although radical land reform was not proposed by the South Carolina body, the cry for the partition of the large estates was raised again and again. An extended debate raged around a proposed stay law designed to prevent the sale of large plantations for debt. R. H. Cain, Negro leader who later served in Congress, opposed the law because it was class legislation which would help the rich only and he favored relieving the poor of both races. F. L. Cardozo, another leading Negro Reconstructionist who was later Secretary of State and State Treasurer, opposed the stay law on the grounds that nine-tenths of the debts on the plantations were contracted for the sale of slaves. By taking this opportunity to throw the plantations upon the market, he held, they would be striking at the plantation system by breaking up the estates and selling them in small lots to the freedmen. "One of the greatest bulwarks of slavery was the plantation system," he declared. "This is the only way by which we will break up that system, and I maintain that our freedom will be of no effect if we allow it to continue. ... Give them an opportunity, breathing time, and they will reorganize the same old system that they had before the war. I say, then ... now is the time to strike." The speaker, however, made it clear that he did not mean confiscation, the only effective measure which would have assured the destruction of the estates. "Let the lands of the South be divided," he said. "I would not say for one moment that they should be confiscated, but if sold to maintain the war, now that slavery is abolished, let the plantation system go with it." The proposal to sell out the large plantation owners was repeated often in this and later bodies.

The convention did not take a definite stand for wholesale confiscation. J. H. Rainey, Negro Republican leader later elected to the House of Representatives, introduced a resolution, which was accepted, whose purpose was "to disabuse the minds of all persons whatsoever throughout the State who may be expecting a distribution of land by the Government of the United States." The resolution stated that it was the belief of the Convention that such distribution never would take place, and "that the only manner in which any land can be obtained by the landless will be by purchase." [9] Even the most advanced Reconstruction body was not ready to press the most fundamental demand of the freedmen.

The convention, however, legislated in favor of the small farmers and thus established a basis of coöperation between the Black Belt and the up-lands. It exempted from forced sales all lands and buildings valued below $1,000 and provided that state lands be sold in tracts not exceeding 160 acres to all classes of the community. Another resolution which received gen-

eral support urged petitioning Congress for a loan of
$1,000,000 with which to purchase land for resale at a
low price.

The proceedings of the other conventions were of
equal interest and varied according to local conditions,
but it is unnecessary to describe them in detail. They
were the initial political bodies of the revolutionary
régimes, reflecting in their composition and activities
the nature of the popular movement, and suffering the
limitations of the bourgeois revolution. If they failed
to take more decisive action on the land question and
more extreme precautions against members of the old
ruling class, these were the weaknesses of a revolution
led by a highly developed bourgeoisie which already
felt the impact of new class conflicts and which at the
same time suffered from legalism and constitution-
alism.

The Fight for the Constitutions

THUS far the new state constitutions were only on
paper and each of the democratic rights proclaimed
in convention still had to be won in action and guaranteed by the state power. The battle raged daily
outside the convention halls. To the Bourbons the seriousness and thoroughness of the revolutionary process
were now fully apparent and they mustered all their
forces. The political campaign now centered around the
plebiscite on the ratification of the new constitutions,
the election of the state governments and of representatives to Congress. The reactionaries dropped the tac-
tic of boycott which had proved unsuccessful in the
elections for the conventions, and began the earnest
organization of opposition parties and extra-legal terroristic bands on a large scale.

The temper of the revolutionary struggle is revealed

in a remarkable speech made by a Negro named Alfred Gray at Uniontown, Alabama, on the eve of the elections for the Constitution which were to take place February 4, 1868. Uniontown is situated in Tallapoosa County, on the fringe of the Alabama Black Belt. Tallapoosa will be remembered as the county where the present Sharecroppers' Union originated in 1931, and as the scene of two bloody struggles between members of the Union and posses of sheriffs and planters at Camp Hill and Reeltown. At Camp Hill, Ralph Gray, a leader of the Union, was murdered in cold blood by members of the posse. Ralph Gray, if not a blood relative, was certainly a spiritual descendant of the Alfred Gray who spoke for the Constitution in the same county some sixty years before.

His speech was reported by the *Independent Monitor,* one of the vilest of reactionary newspapers, published at Tuskaloosa, Alabama. Its editorial policy, it proclaimed, was to "cultivate a Christian disposition towards all except nigger-worshippers whom the Holy Apostles would have considered human monstrosities had they lived in their day." A few months later, one reads, its editor was being pursued by Federal cavalry. This by way of introduction to Alfred Gray's speech, as reported in this paper, for his remarks were undoubtedly distorted. Nevertheless, this version of his speech we will reproduce here, for even in this form it shows how sharply the issues of the revolution were felt by the masses, and what heated resistance such activities roused in the Bourbons. "It is surprising indeed," stated the *Monitor* in its preface to the speech, "that somebody did not blow his head off during this infernal oratorical performance." But his words were flavored in the authentic spirit of the revolution which the Bourbon editor, try as hard as he might, could not sour.

The Constitution, I came here to talk for it—said Alfred Gray—If I get killed I will talk for it. I am not afraid to fight for it, and I will fight for it until hell freezes over. I afraid to fight the white men for my rights? No! I may go to hell, my home is hell, but the white man shall go there with me.

Gentlemen, I am no nigger, I am neither white nor black. Will some one be smart enough to tell me what race I belong to? (Here Frank, as black as tar, said: "Mr. Gray, you is a white man's son by a black 'oman," and another black Negro said, "Yes, and if your mother had been as honest as mine, you'd been as black as I is!") Yes, that's my stock; and my father, god damn his soul to hell, had 300 niggers, and his son sold me for $1,000. Was this right? No! I feel the damned spirit of damnation in me and will fight for our rights until every rascal who chased niggers with hounds is in hell.

Gentlemen, you hear a good deal about social equality, and black and white children going to school together. Well, ain't that right? We pay our $1.50, and make them pay tax on the land that you cleared and which you have the best right to. Then send all to school together. Didn't you clear the white folks' land?

Many voices: "Yes, and we have a right to it!"

Yes, you is, but let them keep it until Congress gives it to us. We have got Congress at our backs and General Grant has turned Radical, and will make the Army give us our rights. What can the white man do when General Grant and General Meade and Congress is on our side?

Well, I will tell you. They have to stop taking the niggers' corn and cotton. You work and make a crop, and the white man takes it for what you owe him, when you ain't seen $20 for a year. But he says, "You took it for your family way back in the summer." Well, you go to the Freedmen's Bureau, and the Bureau man says, "he had a mortgage on your crop," but I know the law, and a mortgage can't take your corn and cotton, for General Meade says, "no matter what a nigger owes you can't take his crop." It is all a lie, boys. The Bureau never did anything but cheat you, and you are poorer now than you were when you were set free. Boys, won't you fight for your rights?

The speaker continued for more than an hour and was loudly applauded. He closed by saying:

Boys, now I want you to hear. Remember the 4th of February. And every one come in and bring your guns and stand up for your rights! Let them talk of social equality, mixed schools and a war of races. We'll fight until we die, and go to hell together, or we'll carry this constitution.

Gray concluded amidst much excitement and was lifted aloft by the crowd who swore they "would fight until they died." [10]
This speech of an ex-slave, probably denied even the rudiments of an elementary education, who had been sold by his own brother as if he were a full-blooded colt, is a revelation of the popular revolution as it unfolded itself among the masses. The deep, undying hatred of their former masters made the freedmen a thoroughly reliable bulwark against counter-revolution. The burning desire for education and for other benefits of democracy transformed them into the driving force of historical progress in the South. And then this ever-recurrent refrain: land, land, land! How typical was Alfred Gray's reply, which reflected the faith of the Negro masses in the Army, in Congress, in the North generally! The North had defeated the slave-masters, abolished slavery, decreed equal rights for them, provided for a democratic transformation of the old oligarchic states. Why, indeed, should it not give them the land? And yet, this faith was not blind. It was based upon past and present accomplishments and it could clearly distinguish betrayal when it occurred,

as in the case of the Freedmen's Bureau, which worked hand in hand with the planters to maintain plantation forced labor and peonage. But they would fight unto death for their rights and carry the constitution which embodied them. "Remember the 4th of February!"

To such ringing cries, often engaging in a real battle of the polls, the Negro masses, supported by sections of the small white agrarians and the urban middle class, voted the constitutions in seven of the ten states by midsummer 1868. The legislatures elected by them passed the Fourteenth Amendment as required in the Reconstruction Acts. By July, Arkansas, North Carolina, South Carolina, Georgia, Alabama, Florida and Louisiana were admitted to representation in Congress upon the condition that they never amend their constitutions to deprive the new electorate of the franchise. Later, Georgia was denied representation in Congress because it expelled the Negro members of the state legislature and held Negroes ineligible for state office. The constitutions had been defeated in Mississippi and Texas at the first plebiscite and the commanding general blocked the election in Virginia. Revised constitutions, omitting the drastic and objectionable clauses disqualifying Confederates, were ratified in these states towards the end of 1869 and they were readmitted by March 1870.

The formal procedure of Reconstruction had been completed, but the struggle had by no means been ended.

Negro Representation in the New Governments

THE high point of the revolution in the South was the extension of civil and political rights to Negroes and their participation in government. Other democratic reforms were made, such as the establishment of a pub-

"**ONE VOTE LESS.**"—*Richmond Whig.*

Cartoon by Nast in *Harpers Weekly*, Sept. 5, 1868.

lic school system and the reorganization of state and county government permitting fuller political activity to white small-farmers. But Negro suffrage and participation in government was undoubtedly the most important innovation of the revolution.

The Negroes, however, did not hold the dominant position in any of the state governments, even in those states where they formed the majority of the electorate. The Reconstruction Governments were maintained for varying periods only as long as the alliance between the Negro people and the up-land farmers existed and was not disrupted by the reaction. From the start the Negroes were handicapped by totally inadequate representation in the state and national governments. Even in South Carolina, where the revolution reached its highest level, the Negroes did not dominate the state power. They were in the great majority in the Lower House of the three legislatures which met between 1868 and 1873 and the number of their representatives was only slightly less than the white in the two Houses which sat between 1874 and 1878. But at all times the whites maintained a majority in the Senate and controlled the governor's office. Negroes held other state offices: they served as Lieutenant-Governors of the state twice; two held the post of Speaker of the House for four years; one was Secretary of State and State Treasurer, another served as Adjutant and Inspector General; and seven Negroes were elected to Congress at various times. Although the Negro people played a decisive rôle in maintaining these governments and in initiating and carrying through democratic reforms, the administration was largely in the hands of their Northern and Southern allies.

In Mississippi and Louisiana, the two other states in which Negroes were in the majority of the population, Negro representation was even less. In the first Reconstruction legislature of Louisiana about half the representatives in the Lower House were Negroes but they had only seven Senators. Their representation was decreased in the later bodies of the state. Of other offices during the period, there were three Negro Lieutenant-Governors, a Secretary of State, State Treasurer and Superintendent of Public Education and one Negro Congressman. Lieutenant-Governor P. B. S. Pinchback served as Governor during an interim period of 43 days, the only Negro to hold that office in the South.

There were never more than 9 Negroes out of 35 members in the Senate and 55 out of 115 members in the Lower House of the Mississippi legislature. In this state, according to a Negro Conservative who wished to minimize the rôle of the Negro, a Negro never occupied a judicial post higher than Justice of the Peace. Of seven state officers, only one, that of Secretary of State, was filled by a Negro until 1873, when colored men were also elected as Lieutenant-Governor and Superintendent of Education. No more than one Negro Representative or Senator sat in Congress at any one time. Unlike the situation in South Carolina and Louisiana, where Negroes held many of the county offices, in the 72 counties of Mississippi which elected on an average 28 officers to a county, not more than five out of 100 were Negroes. "The state, district, county and municipal governments," wrote the Conservative Negro leader, "were not only in control of white men, but white men who were to the manor born, or who were known as old citizens of the state." [11]

In the other states, Negro representation in the legislature was even less. The post of the superintendent of education was filled by a Negro in many states, eloquent testimony to the striving of the illiterate freedmen for education. Between 1871 and 1901, there were 22 Negro members of Congress, two of whom were Senators.

Today, when government in the South is based upon white domination and the ostracism of the Negro, and when there is only one Negro representative in Congress, these facts may appear startling. In one sense they are: they reveal an active participation of the freedmen and their representatives in democratic government only a few years after the abolition of slavery and, as events showed, they exerted a powerful progressive influence. This is one of the rare instances in history when an enslaved peasant people so quickly and so effectively, within the limitations of the time and the revolution, rose to participate in state power. On the other hand, it is clear that democracy even during this revolutionary epoch had worked itself out only partially. At the height of popular democracy in the South the Negro was still inadequately represented in the assemblies and in the offices of power. This was an important contributing factor to the defeat of the Reconstruction governments.

To the Bourbons the participation of the Negro in government, even to the smallest degree, was already "Negro Domination." One Negro legislator immediately was multiplied in their startled eyes to a hundred. The Bourbon press raged in the vilest terms against the "Black Parliaments." Even in the sanest of their papers, the vituperation and calumny heaped upon the "white and black niggers" did not flatter the "brains and intelligence" which was said to be the peculiar attribute of the old ruling class. It certainly rankled to have their former slaves, or even some of their working field hands, pass some of the most progressive legislation the South has ever had, or tax the rich to provide an education for the poor. "Negro

Domination" became the shibboleth of counter-revolution, the political slogan under which the reactionaries rallied the poor white masses against the revolution. This is the way the myth of "Negro Domination" was born, and it is in the Bourbon press that most of our historians discovered it.

If anything, the Reconstruction governments suffered from insufficient domination by the democratic classes over the old rulers.

The "Black Parliaments"

THE revolution struck home most thoroughly in South Carolina, Mississippi and Louisiana and in these states the "Black Parliaments" were more completely assemblies of the people. The social composition of the first South Carolina Reconstruction legislature, 84 of whose 157 members were Negroes, is revealed by the fact that the taxes paid by all the legislators amounted to $700.63, of which six members paid $309.01. There were not many men of property here. But property, in the person of a Black Belt plantation owner, looked down from the balcony and declared in amazement: "My God, look at this!" Negroes who but three years before had been slaves were legislating for the public welfare.

Through the eyes of James S. Pike, a leading Northern Republican who visited South Carolina and returned home to launch a campaign of slander and vituperation against the Reconstruction governments, we can at least catch a glimpse of the legislature of 1873. Only a revolution in which the widest masses are set in motion can produce such a parliamentary body. Despite Pike's condescending jibes, even from his description of the members of the assembly as they left the State House, it is apparent that this was primarily an assembly of landless peasants and small land-owners:

About three-quarters of the crowd belonged to the African race. They were of every hue, from the octoroon to the deep black. They were such a good looking body of men as might pour out of a market house or a courthouse at random in any Southern state. Every Negro type and physiognomy was here to be seen, from the genteel serving man to the rough hewn customer from rice or cotton field. Their dress was as varied as their countenances. There was the second-hand frock coat of infirm gentility, glossy and threadbare. There was the stovepipe hat of many ironings and departed styles. There was also to be seen a total disregard of the proprieties of costume in the coarse and dirty garments of the field; the stub-jackets and slouch hats of soiling labor. In some instances, rough woolen comforters embraced the neck and hid the absence of linen. Heavy brogans and short, torn trousers it was impossible to hide.... These were the legislators of South Carolina.

Pike had never seen the like of it in any Northern state, where legislators were men of property and "substantial citizens." He was even more alarmed at the leading rôle of the Negroes in the legislature. Sessions were opened by a chaplain who was "coal black"; the Chairman of the House Committee of Ways and Means was "another full black man"; two of the best speakers in the House were "quite black, both leaders rather than led." In the Senate, Beverly Nash, formerly a slave and later a bootblack in one of the hotels, towered above every one else. "Go into the Senate," continued Pike. "It is not too much to say that the leading man of the Republican Party in that body is Beverly Nash, a man wholly black. He is apparently consulted more and appealed to more, in the business of the body, than any man in it. It is admitted by his white opposition colleagues that he has more native

ability than half the white men in the Senate." The
Senator from Georgetown "boasts of being a Negro,
and of having no fear of the white man in any respect.
He evidently has no love for them.... He appears to
be one of the leading 'strikers,' and is not led except
through his interests." A young Negro member of the
House told Pike that the "lawyers and the white
chivalry, as they call themselves" have learned to let
Beverly Nash alone. "When he undertakes a thing, he
generally puts it through, I tell you. No sir, there is
nobody who cares to attack Beverly Nash. They will
let him alone right smart."

The Northerner, accustomed to the finished perora-
tions and well-turned phrases of constitutional lawyers
in sedate legislative bodies, was taken aback at the
home-spun fashion in which this people's body conducted its business, although he could not help but
sense their intense seriousness.

The leading topics of discussion—wrote Pike—are all well
understood by the members, as they are of practical character, and appeal directly to the personal interests of every
legislator, as well as those of his constituents. When an
appropriation bill is up to raise money to catch and punish
the K.K.K., they know exactly what it means.... So, too,
with educational measures. The free school comes right
home to them; then the business of arming and drilling the
black militia. They are eager on this point.

The laughing propensity of the sable crowd is a great
cause of disorder.... But underneath all this shocking
burlesque upon legislative proceedings, we must not forget
that there is something real to this uncouth and untutored
multitude. It is not all sham, nor all burlesque. They have a
genuine interest and a genuine earnestness in the business of
the assembly which we are bound to recognize and respect.
... They have an earnest purpose born of a conviction that
their position and condition are not fully assured, which
lends a sort of dignity to their proceedings.

Their position and condition were certainly not fully assured. Outside the legislative chambers, a constant battle waged: therefore the eagerness about suppressing the K.K.K. and maintaining the Negro militias, an eagerness which surprised our observer, for he did not seem to realize that the masses in their "uncouth" and unrefined manner have the talent for self-government.

Pike was also surprised to find that the Negro leaders were not led by the nose by white Republicans. "The black man of the legislature feels his oats," he observed, "and considers that the time has already arrived when he can take care of himself." The Negro Republicans would not throw away their Party advantages but would use them for their own purposes. In the Party caucuses and in the Union Leagues, where legislative affairs were shaped, the white leaders, according to Pike, did not hold sway. He cites the action of the legislature on a number of occasions to bear out his view.[12]

An example of supreme historical justice was the election of Hiram R. Revels, a Negro minister, to fill the unexpired term of Jefferson Davis in Congress. The political revolution was typified in the election of former slaves to high legislative posts: Oscar J. Dunn, a runaway slave and later a house painter, was President of the Senate in Louisiana and Lieutenant-Governor of the State; five of fourteen Negro members of Reconstruction Congresses were born slaves. A Northern observer visiting the Mississippi assembly in 1873 told how the Negro members had voluntarily taken their seats on one side of the house, while the Conservatives were gathered at the extreme right. Whenever a Conservative proposed any measure he was greeted by a deafening chorus of "Mr. Speaker!" from the left side. The proceedings were "enlivened by the occasional outburst of a dusky member, who fiercely disputed the floor with his ex-master." [13]

Most of the Negro leaders in the Reconstruction governments were men who had received education and training in the Abolition movement. Quite a number were Northerners who had come South with the Union troops as soldiers, ministers, teachers or agents of the Freedmen's Bureau. New Orleans supplied many leaders who had been free colored men of property under slavery. There were not a few Negro mechanics and artisans, who either as free or slave workers had had the opportunity under slavery for self-education.

The Negro in Local Government

NEGROES were also energetic in municipal and county affairs. In the very verbose but sketchy account of a trip through the Southern states during the whole of 1873 and the spring and summer of 1874, Edward King, a writer for *Scribners*, who might be characterized as an honest but pedantic conservative Republican, gives a passing view of the local situation. At Petersburg, Virginia, where the Negroes outnumbered the whites, they were largely represented on the Common Council and sometimes had a controlling voice in municipal affairs. At Little Rock, Arkansas, there were two Negro aldermen who had been slaves up to the war and quite a number of the counties in the State had Negro sheriffs and clerks. In Houston, Texas, some members of the City Council and the supervisor of streets were Negroes.

King attended a session of a parish jury in Vidalia, Louisiana, near Natchez, and found it nearly all composed of Negroes. The functions of the jury were similar to those of county commissioners in Northern states and the planters complained bitterly that "nine out of ten who sit upon the jury are ignorant and have no property and yet are permitted to judge what is best for the interests of property holders." At Natchez, in the heart of the Delta Black Belt, the sheriff, the county treasurer and assessor, the majority of the magistrates, and all the officers managing county affairs, except one, were Negroes. For the first time in the history of the county, public schools had been established and one handsome new schoolhouse was called "Union."

King also visited the coastal and Sea Islands region of South Carolina where he found the "revolution penetrated to the quick." At Beaufort, the center of this overwhelmingly Negro area, the city hall was entirely controlled by Negroes and the magistrates, the police and the representatives to the legislature were practically all Negroes. He found most of the men armed, "desirous of seeing the lands in the commonwealth" in the hands of their own people, and "impressed with the idea that South Carolina should be in some measure a black man's government." [14]

The same area was visited in 1879, after the counterrevolutionary *coup d'état,* by Sir George Campbell, a Member of Parliament, and he was surprised to find that the Negroes had maintained many of their gains. Although their title to the land was then again being attacked, they had established independent and self-supporting rural communities, while many of the men also worked in the ports and the phosphate beds. At Beaufort the Negroes still controlled the elections and sent their own people to the municipal and county offices, as well as representatives to the State Assembly. "It has the reputation of being a sort of black paradise," wrote Campbell about the Beaufort area, "and *per contra,* I rather expected a white hell.... To my great surprise I found exactly the contrary. At no place that I have seen are the relations of the races better and more peaceable." [15]

The energetic participation of the Negro in politics was certainly a complete reversal of the old situation. In the words of a ditty current among the Negroes of South Carolina:

"De bottom rail's on de top,
An' we's gwine to keep it dar."

Bourgeois Reforms and "Corruption"

THE work of the legislative bodies was limited by the nature of the alliance which sustained them and by the capitalist property relationships which necessarily served as a basis. But within these limits the Reconstruction legislatures, especially in those states where the Negroes played a leading rôle, undertook progressive and democratic measures. The new legislation was generally along the lines laid down by the Reconstruction Constitutions and covered (1) civil rights for Negroes, including the ratification of the Fourteenth and Fifteenth Amendments; (2) the establishment of a public school system; (3) reorganization of state and county government; (4) revision of the system of taxation; (5) land and labor relations; and (6) aid to railroads and other capitalist undertakings. The extent of such legislation and its enforcement depended upon the level of the revolution in the various states. In some cases the Radical governments lasted only two or three years: in Virginia, North Carolina and Georgia, conservatives and reactionaries already controlled the state by the end of 1870. In still others, such as Alabama and Texas, the Radicals had only a slight edge on the Conservatives.

Black Codes and the old slave laws were repealed and in most cases Civil Rights Bills were passed to enforce equal rights for Negroes on conveyances and in public institutions. When the Civil Rights Bill passed in Louisiana, a Bourbon paper warned "any Negro, or gang of Negroes" attempting to exercise the privileges it conferred would do so "at their peril." The mere passage of such measures did not assure equal rights and many were the battles waged by Negroes to maintain the rights conferred by their legislatures. For example, when the Common Carrier Bill, providing for equal accommodations on street cars and railroads, was before the Alabama body, hundreds of Negroes and a number of their white allies held demonstrations against the street cars in Mobile (which discriminated against Negroes) and boarded all the cars.[16]

The Negro members of the state assemblies were naturally most adamant in fighting for equal rights. When the Civil Rights Bill was before the Alabama session of 1872-73, the Negro representative Merriwether declared that his people intended to assert their rights everywhere. In reply to a conservative who charged that Negroes wished to use these rights as stepping-stones to something beyond, he declared: "They are stepping-stones, and the colored people intend stepping along upon them until they stand side by side with the gentlemen who oppose them." Mr. Lewis of Perry, a Black Belt county, warned the Republican Party that the Negro people intended to hold them to their platform and their promises.[17]

In the first Reconstruction legislature of Louisiana, where the Republican majority was small, Oscar J. Dunn, Negro president of the Senate, and R. H. Isbelle, Negro chairman of the Lower House, led a vigorous fight to require the Democratic delegates to take the "iron-clad oath" before seating them. The oath required of all those taking office that they swear they had never borne arms against the government of the

United States or supported the Confederacy. It was much more stringent than the provisions of the Fourteenth Amendment disqualifying former Confederates, and was aimed at the counter-revolutionists who had found their way into the legislature. The Negroes were so firm in their demand that soldiers were massed outside the State House for protection. Grant forced a compromise by having the Democrats take the constitutional oath only. Ficklen, the historian of Reconstruction in the state, says of this incident:

It showed a disposition on the part of the Negroes and their white allies to adopt a more radical program in their treatment of the whites than General Grant himself would authorize, and forecasted a determination to legislate wholly with reference to their own interests.[18]

In Georgia, the Negroes waged an unequal struggle against a strong Conservative alignment, which included a number of anti-Radical Republicans. The first legislature refused to seat the Negro members on the ground that Negroes were not eligible for office in the state. The Negro Republicans met in militant convention at Macon "to inaugurate war against the foul and base action of the so-called Legislature and to oppose the principles of all men who oppose equal rights." [19] With the aid of Congress, which refused to seat Georgia members until the right of Negroes to hold office was recognized, Negro members resumed their seats in a legislature which was already under the control of reactionaries. The Negroes formed the Left of the assembly and pressed a number of progressive measures, such as bills for female suffrage and prison reform. The latter was directed against the practice of leasing out convicts to private contractors.

A common school system was established, for which the Negro delegates in the legislatures fought the hardest and which they insisted on maintaining at all costs. As long as they had a voice in the state governments these systems were maintained for both whites and Negroes. As soon as the reactionaries began to get the upper hand, they were curtailed as, for example, in Alabama where the schools were closed down because funds could "not be found" to pay teachers.

The class nature of the new Reconstruction governments is best illustrated by the new system of taxation which was instituted by them. The public school system, the democratic reorganization of state and county administration, and public improvements such as new roads, bridges, charitable institutions and state buildings, greatly increased the expenses of government. Historians who mechanically repeat Bourbon charges of extravagance against the Reconstruction governments, forget that there were no such public items of expense under the slave oligarchy. The establishment of the schools constituted one of the largest items in the state budget and was a social duty of which the old slavemasters knew nothing. To them it was foolish extravagance to supply free education to "poor whites" and Negroes, to provide funds for the election of county officers (who were generally appointed under the oligarchy), to establish asylums for the handicapped, etc. It was considered even greater squandering and corruption when the new governments set about raising these funds from among all men of property, including the big planters. While fraud undoubtedly existed, especially in connection with railroad subsidies, the cry of corruption was a political weapon used against the legislatures which carried through measures for the public welfare on funds raised by taxing the planters.

This becomes evident when the methods of taxation before and after the war are compared. In South Caro-

lina, for example, the system before the war placed a
low valuation on land and slaves and taxed heavily
the merchants, professionals and bankers. The middle
class businessmen paid taxes five and six times as great
as the planter. When the planters were overthrown
and the middle class controlled the state power, the
situation was changed. The system of taxation was
revised on a uniform basis applying to all property at
its full value. The rate of taxation was increased to
meet the new needs of democratic government and
additional increases were necessitated by the fact that
assessed property values had fallen drastically. In
many states, taxation supplied insufficient revenue,
especially when the planters instituted an economic
boycott and refused to pay taxes, forcing the administration to borrow and increase the state debt.

The planter interests raised a continual cry that the
"carpetbag-scalawag-Negro" governments wanted to
raise taxes to the point of confiscation. And why not?
Having failed to obtain land by outright confiscation
of the estates, the Negroes pressed for higher taxation
of the large landowner to force him to work all his
land, since he could not afford to let it lie idle, or sell
parcels of it to the landless freedmen and whites, if not
force him into bankruptcy altogether. As we have seen,
the Negro leaders at the South Carolina Constitutional
Convention, fought against the stay law hoping in
this way to force the planters to sell and break up the
large estates. In the Alabama assembly, the Negro
delegates pressed for an equalization board, which
would revalue the land at a higher rate. Lewis, a Negro
member, declared that the taxes on land in the plantation counties ought to be raised to such a point that
the large landowners would be compelled to sell so
that Negroes could buy. The reactionary forces rallied
on this issue. "All this is more horrible than true," de-

clared the editor of the *Southern Argus,* one of the milder of the planters' organs. "If the State of Alabama remains in the hands of the Radical party a short while longer, our boys will be the bootblacks and our girls the washer-women of those bloated pieces of human corruption who stalk with such lordly air through this land and are called public officials." [20]

Taxation became the leading economic issue in the Reconstruction states. Many planters were actually forced to forfeit land for taxes or to sell at a low price. In Mississippi, for instance, 640,000 acres of land were sold for taxes. Land values fell as much as 65% and 75% in Alabama and Louisiana, and to half in several other states.[21] This was also due to other causes besides the higher rate of taxation.* But the sale of large tracts of land at low prices offered the Negro to some extent an opportunity to buy, although it also led to much land speculation and the establishment of absentee ownership over large plantations.

Some measures of the new state assemblies also extended the opportunity for landless farm workers to purchase land. In South Carolina a land commission was established to purchase land and sell it in lots of from 25 to 100 acres to actual settlers; $500,000 was raised for this purpose. By 1871, nearly 2,000 small farms were occupied or ready to be settled. A limited class of Negro small landowners was thus established under Reconstruction.

* The transformation of the Southern agrarian system during this period, as well as unfavorable economic conditions generally, led to the decline in land values and to the bankruptcy of sections of the planters. The abolition of slavery deprived the largest planters of most of their capital which had been invested in slaves, while the war left the South without ready capital or credit. In addition, the labor supply remained disorganized pending the establishment on a profitable basis, with the aid of Northern capital, of plantation tenancy and the credit merchant system.

A large portion of the debts incurred by the states was in connection with the extension of aid to railroads. Subsidies amounting to as high as $16,000 a mile were extended for the construction of the roads. As in the North, speculation was rife in the state railroad bonds and New York brokerage houses got most of the profits. Railroad lobbies in the Southern legislatures probably did grease the palm of many a lawmaker and state officer. But this graft and corruption among public officials was not the monopoly of the Southern Reconstruction governments nor the attribute of "Negro Domination," as the reactionaries charged. The *Credit Mobilier* railroad scandals in the North, land speculation, gold manipulation and other forms of corruption involving a vice-president and a number of Congressmen * made the Southerners look like "small timers." In states like Georgia, Alabama and North Carolina, where railroad mileage was more than doubled during this period and where the native whites controlled the governments, the subsidies were the highest. After all, it was a bourgeois-democratic revolution and the governments were *bourgeois*-democratic, with all the vices of such governments, including graft and corruption, during a period of boom and the rapid development of capitalism. Railroads were necessary to the development of the interior markets and of industry, and the Reconstruction governments set about supplying this

---

* A congressional investigation revealed that the *Credit Mobilier*, construction company of the Union Pacific Railroad, engaged in fraud and bribery involving a number of Congressmen and public officials. Vice-President Colfax accepted stocks of the company practically as a gift. President Grant's private secretary was implicated in the "Whiskey Ring" of St. Louis, which defrauded the government out of millions of dollars in taxes. Secretary of War Belknap was involved in the Indian agencies scandals. In New York, a Democratic stronghold, William ("Boss") Tweed, in alliance with Tammany, stole from the City a sum variously estimated at from $50,000,000 to $200,000,000.

need in the best way capitalist government knew how.

The cry of corruption was at best only a political slogan with the aid of which the Bourbons sought to regain state power.

Certainly, the Reconstruction governments established the basis for democratic legislation in the South and some of their outstanding innovations, such as the democratization of administrative machinery and the public school system, still stand. But in their comment upon the work of the Reconstructionists, the leading Bourbon newspapers give the impression of having suddenly gone crazy. The *Fairfield* (S. C.) *Herald*, for example, characterized the policy of the Reconstruction legislature as

a hell-born policy which has trampled the fairest and noblest of states of our great sisterhood beneath the unholy hoofs of African savages and shoulder-strapped brigands—the policy which has given up millions of our free-born, high-souled brothers and sisters, countrymen and countrywomen of Washington, Rutledge, Marion and Lee, to the rule of gibbering, louse-eaten, devil-worshipping barbarians, from the jungles of Dahomey, and peripatetic buccaneers from Cape Cod, Memphremagog, Hell and Boston.[22]

"Spirit(s) of the Democratic Party."—*Harpers Weekly*, Aug. 22, 1868.

CHAPTER VI

THE LABOR MOVEMENT

Resurgence of the Trade Unions

THE rapid development of industry during the Civil War decade was accompanied by a resurgence and advance of the labor movement. The promising labor movement of the 'thirties and 'forties had been submerged by the dominant social crisis. The economic depression of 1857 practically eliminated the remaining unions. At the outbreak of war there were only four national unions in more than nominal existence. As the war stimulated industrial activity and as production began to shift from a domestic to a factory basis, local unions quickly reappeared. They united into city central bodies or "trades' assemblies." When the central labor unions met nationally at the convention of the Industrial Assembly of North America in 1864 the trade unions already claimed 200,000 members.

An extensive eight-hour movement was initiated at the same time. The demand was raised for a uniform reduction in the working day to eight hours, without decrease in wages. Eight-Hour Leagues sprang up everywhere and were almost as numerous as the local unions. The principal strength of the movement was in the Northeast, but it also penetrated the South. "The leaven of the North has already begun to work in the South," moaned a Bourbon newspaper reporting a mass meeting for the eight-hour day called by the Mechanics' Association of New Orleans. The meeting, held in March 1866, was among the first in the South and announced that the workers were advancing to maintain their rights "against the oppression of capital." The newspaper feared that Negro suffrage would be given to sustain these "new and enlightened views of the dignity of labor." [1] A large mass meeting called by the Caulkers' and Ship Carpenters' Union was held a week later in Mobile and adopted a resolution calling for united action to obtain the shorter work day. [2] The "New England controversies," as Southern papers dubbed the labor problem, appeared upon the scene early. Within a few years the national movement for the shorter work day became powerful enough to cause the passage of eight-hour laws by some municipal councils and by six state legislatures. In 1868, a Federal act was passed providing for the eight-hour day for government laborers, workmen and mechanics. The law, however, was generally rendered a dead letter by the government's farming out work to contractors, who were not covered by the legislation.

Economic conditions in the North sped class stratification and the opening of the modern phase of the labor movement. War prosperity was strictly the property of the upper class. The workers were worse off than before the outbreak of hostilities. Although wages in inflated currency had risen, the advance in wages did not keep pace with the advance in prices. A leading Republican newspaper had to admit in September 1864 that while the cost of living had doubled, "wages are only from 12 to 20 per cent higher than they were before the war and there is absolute want in many families, while thousands of young children who should be at school are shut up at work that they may earn something to eke out the scant supplies at home." In Congress it was stated that "there stalks through every great city the gaunt wolf of hunger and distress." A committee appointed by the Senate during the last year of the war to investigate wages and prices reported that wages, measured in gold, fell off rapidly until in 1865 they stood at about one-third less than in 1860.[3] The wages of women workers were especially meager. In 1861 the government was paying 17½ cents for making shirts and in 1864 the wage in comparative values was six cents, while contractors were paying only half this amount.[4] Prices leaped skyward: butter rose from 12 to 64 cents a pound between 1861 and 1864, eggs from 8 to 52 cents a dozen, potatoes from $1 to $6.50 a bushel; flour from $4 to $10.50 a barrel; sugar from 5 to 22 cents a pound.[5]

To resist the onslaught upon their living standards, while fortunes were being created at the top, the workers turned to the organization of unions and struggle. In the midst of the bourgeois revolution, the fundamental class struggle of the capitalist era again emerged on a much more extensive scale and on a broader basis than before. During the last year of war, the workers experienced a bitter foretaste of bourgeois reaction. The steps taken by the military command in St. Louis in April 1864 to smash strikes of blacksmiths, machinists and tailors indicated the rupture of the war alliance between basically antagonistic classes. Under pretense of safeguarding the Union, Military Order No. 65 prohibited the organization of labor unions and picketing, and guaranteed military protection to factories employing strikebreakers. Several labor union men, who were also Loyal Unionists, were arrested under this order. Similar steps against strikers were taken in Louisville, Kentucky, by a general who was said to be "in the confidence of the employers, aware of all their plans and objects." The military ukase in this case was almost identical with Order No. 65, even to terminology, and indicated a general policy emanating from Washington. At Cold Springs, New

York, Federal troops were used to break a strike in a munition plant where the workers were demanding an increase in wages. A number of strikers were arrested, held without trial, and then forced to leave the town under threat.

Immediate and widespread demonstrations and protests by workers prevented the passage of a Bill, introduced in the New York legislature in 1864, terming all labor union members criminals, subject to imprisonment for one year and a fine of $250. A timely demonstration of the Boston workers also prevented the final passage of a similar bill in Massachusetts, after it had already passed one branch of the state legislature. Through government interference, the Miners' Association in the eastern coal fields of Pennsylvania was broken and the Reading railroad engineers were defeated. The back pay of the molders in the Brooklyn navy yard was confiscated when they struck for higher wages. Convict labor was introduced at Sing Sing.

These and other developments during the war tested the patience of loyal labor leaders such as William H. Sylvis, president of the Molders' Union and outstanding exponent of a national organization of labor. Citing the acts of the employers and the government against the workers in a speech at Chicago on January 9, 1865, Sylvis declared:

In ordinary times a collision would have been inevitable. Nothing but the patient patriotism of the people, and their desire in no way to embarrass the government, prevent it. But "there is a point where forebearance ceases to be a virtue,"—that point *may* be reached. [*Italics in original.*][6]

Independent Political Action

WITH the end of the war, the situation matured rapidly to the point where Sylvis' prophecy came to life. The resurgent labor movement headed quickly towards national organization. The formation of a national labor party, independent of the two chief parties, was being argued on all sides. In a book on the labor movement, written in the heyday of the Knights of Labor, McNeill referred to the upsurge in the workers' ranks in 1866 and remarked that "the people of today have little conception of the extent of the labor movement of twenty years ago." [7] The first nation-wide organization of trade unions in the modern period was formed only one year after the end of the war. The inaugural session of the National Labor Union took place in August 1866 in response to a call which placed eight hours at the head of labor's demands and stressed the need for concerted action *"upon all matters appertaining to the inauguration of labor reforms."* The workers were reacting speedily to the needs of the new period and beginning to emerge as an independent class force. In his first volume of *Capital,* published in 1867, Marx summed up the situation with masterly precision:

In the United States of America—he wrote—any sort of independent labor movement was paralyzed so long as slavery disfigured a part of the republic. Labor with a white skin cannot emancipate itself where labor with a black skin is branded. But out of the death of slavery a new and vigorous life sprang. The first fruit of the Civil War was an agitation for the eight-hour day—a movement which ran with express speed from the Atlantic to the Pacific, from New England to California.[8]

At the initial Congress of the National Labor Union, comprising 70 delegates from 13 states, independent political action was the subject of heated debate from the moment Schlëgel, a German Socialist of Chicago, introduced a motion for the formation of a labor party.

The Congress endorsed the idea. In an Address issued the following July, which took up the pressing problems facing the labor movement, the National Labor Union called upon the workers to "cut aloof from the ties and trammels of party, manipulated in the interests of capital." Sylvis greeted the first convention as a success but criticized it for not having worked out ways and means of organization and for depending upon spontaneous action to produce results. "If we resort to political action at all," he warned, "we must keep clear of all entangling alliances. With a distinct workingmen's party in the field, there can be no distrust, no want of confidence." [9]

In subsequent conventions the National Labor Union worked out a political platform which already showed the disintegrating influence of petty-bourgeois reform schemes and agrarian greenbackism. Sylvis was elected President at the 1868 Congress, when the Union was at the height of its power and claimed 600,000 members. In a circular announcing the decision of the body to organize the Labor Reform Party "for the purpose of getting control of Congress and the several state legislatures," Sylvis called upon the workers to leave the old parties. "Let our cry be *reform*," he wrote, "—down with a moneyed aristocracy and up with the people!" In another circular, Sylvis pointed out that "there is rapidly building up in this country a privileged money aristocracy, such as nowhere else exists," which not only controls "the productive powers of the nation" but also the government. The people were being divided into two classes—the rich and the poor, the producers and the non-producers.

The working people of our nation—he continued—white and black, male and female, are sinking to a condition of serfdom. Even now a slavery exists in our land worse than ever existed under the old slave system. The center of the slave power no longer exists south of Mason's and Dixon's line. It has been transferred to Wall Street; its vitality is to be found in our huge national bank swindle, and a false monetary system. The war abolished the right of property in man, but it did not abolish slavery. This movement we are now engaged in is the great anti-slavery movement, and we must push on the work of emancipation until slavery is abolished in every corner of our country. Our objective point is a new monetary system, a system that will take from a few men the power to control the money, and give to the people a cheap, secure, and abundant currency. This done, and the people will be free. Then will come such a social revolution as the world has never witnessed. . . .[10]

This circular typifies the advanced position of the National Labor Union. But it also demonstrates the weaknesses which would destroy it. The "financial oligarchy" was seen as the principal enemy, while the rising industrial bourgeoisie, the opponent directly facing labor, was not clearly differentiated. Emphasis was, therefore, wrongly placed upon the monetary aspects of the system with the result that the economic struggles of the workers for higher wages and better conditions found insufficient expression. Political strategy was correctly centered on the organization of an independent labor party, but the political program was erroneous. The money system was blamed for wage-slavery and deliverance was sought in the use of new paper money as legal tender. By the use of the greenback, Sylvis and other labor and farmers' leaders argued, the use of gold as money could be dispensed with, there would no longer be need for bankers and brokers; the workers would be "free from the grasp of the money power."

From the viewpoint of the workers and farmers there was at that time good ground for demanding a reform in the monetary system. The greenbacks issued in 1862 depreciated, while the interest on government bonds was paid in gold. The bankers and brokers hoarded gold at the beginning of the war and later bought up the depreciated greenbacks with gold. They used these greenbacks to buy more government bonds which were redeemable in gold and paid interest in gold. While the workers could buy less and less with their depreciated money a huge swindle was being put over by the "moneyed aristocracy." Therefore, argued the radical greenbackers, do away with gold and thereby do away with Wall Street. But the solution even of the interest swindle did not lie in more inflation. The whole program was erroneous and by 1871 the National Labor Union as a trade union body was already ineffectual and the Labor Reform Party became submerged in the money reform agrarianism.

If Sylvis had had the opportunity to develop further the relations which had already been set up with the International Workingmen's Association, the Labor Party movement might have developed along somewhat different lines. At the 1867 Congress, Sylvis had proposed affiliation of the National Labor Union to the I.W.A. Shortly before his death in July 1869, when war with England threatened, the International sent an Address to Sylvis as president of the National Labor Union *, in which the relationship of class forces resulting from the Civil War was clearly defined. It was pointed out that the Civil War had "offered compensation in the liberation of the slaves and the impulse which it thereby gave to your own class movement" as evidenced in the beginnings of an independent labor movement. After a clear summation of the import of the Civil War, the Address continued:

Yours, then, is the glorious task of seeing to it that at last the working class shall enter upon the scene of history,

* See Appendices, Document 8.

no longer as a servile following, but as an independent power, as a power imbued with a sense of its responsibility and capable of commanding peace when their would-be masters cry war.

In his reply to the Address, Sylvis again stressed that:

The most infamous money aristocracy of the earth ... saps the very life of the people. We have declared war against it and we are determined to conquer—by means of the ballot, if possible—if not, we shall resort to more serious means. A little blood-letting is necessary in desperate cases.[11]

The movement for independent political action was shunted off into the maze of money reform. But it showed that if the workers had not broken with bourgeois ideology entirely they were at least breaking away organizationally from the bourgeois parties. A large advanced section definitely split away from the Republican Party, the leader of the bourgeois revolution but at the same time the party of the new financial oligarchy and the industrialists.

The National Labor Union and the Negro

THE attitude of the politically awakened labor movement to the questions of Reconstruction was necessarily conditioned by its growing opposition to the Republican Party as the political arm of the industrial and financial aristocracy. By means of a Radical Reconstruction policy the big bourgeoisie was entrenching itself in power. At the same time, a basis for solidarity with the Negro toilers was being sought in the organized labor movement. A strong tendency for solidarity with Negro workers and for alliance with the Negro people made itself felt early.

Less than two percent of the Northern population was Negro. Numerically the Negro workers did not form an important part of the Northern proletariat, although there were some unions of Negro laborers and skilled mechanics at the end of the war. The chief problem of the Negro worker was to overcome numerous discriminations which barred his advance in the skilled trades. In the South there were twice as many Negro mechanics as white. Negro laborers were employed in large numbers in the tobacco, brickmaking and shipcaulking industries, on railroad construction and on the docks. They also began to migrate north. The labor movement was therefore faced with the necessity of defining its attitude to the Negroes already in industry and now entering in larger numbers. The crystallization of a labor movement among the Negro people and their position on independent political action depended largely upon the attitude taken by the organized white workers.

The National Labor Union devoted an important section of its very first Address to the workers, in July 1867, to the question of Negro labor "in the successful solution of which the working classes have an abiding interest." The Negro workers, the Address pointed out, "must necessarily become in their new relationship an element of strength or an element of weakness, and it is for the workingmen of America to decide which that shall be." Citing instances in which employers imported Negro workers from the South during the struggle for the eight-hour day, the National Labor Union asked whether the white workers would permit the capitalists to realize their "cherished idea of antagonism between white and black labor." The question was: "Shall we make them our friends, or shall capital be allowed to turn them as an engine against us?"

Taking this view of the question—continues the Address —we are of the opinion that the interests of the labor cause demand that all workingmen be included within its ranks, without regard to race or nationality; and that the interests of the workingmen of America especially require that the formation of trade unions, eight-hour leagues and other labor organizations, should be encouraged among the colored race; that they be instructed in the true principles of labor reform, and that they be invited to coöperate with us in the general labor undertaking.

The Committee which drew up the Address presented this section as its own position, explaining that it was aware of the differences of opinion among the delegates at the Congress and did not hope to present an opinion which would meet the approval of everybody. However, it urged its own position vigorously. The Address did not set forth the steps to be taken in the organization of Negro labor but such measures, the Committee declared, they were willing to leave "to the decision and wisdom of the next Congress, believing that such enlightened action will be there developed as to redound to the best and most lasting interests of all concerned." [12] On the whole, this was an advanced document to come from the labor movement on a threshold of a period which gives solidarity between white and Negro labor its main content.

The extended debates on this question at the next Congress (Chicago, August 1867) revealed that the main differences of opinion revolved about the admission of Negro workers into the existing trade unions. The Congress was much broader than the first, comprising about 200 delegates from all the Northern states and including delegates from the border states of Kentucky, Maryland and Missouri. The Committee on Negro Labor in its report to the Congress refused to commit itself on the question on the ground that it was too complicated and proposed that it be shelved until the next Congress. Sylvis strongly opposed the recommendation. Postponement would be suicidal, he said, since "this question has already been introduced in the South, the whites striking against the blacks, and creating an antagonism which will kill off the trade unions, unless the two be consolidated." Trevellick, another influential labor leader, and other delegates argued for admitting Negroes into the trade unions as the best means of organizing the Negro workers. But the border states delegates and the representative of the Eight-Hour League of Michigan would have the Negro workers organize trade unions and assemblies among themselves. The Committee finally reported that "after due deliberation the Constitution already adopted by the labor Congress precludes the necessity of any action of this body in behalf of any particular class of the laboring masses." The key question was again evaded at the 1868 Congress, which passed a resolution rejoicing in the abolition of slavery and inviting the "working classes of the South" to join the movement.

The 1869 Congress of the National Labor Union was an historic occasion if for no other reason than the participation of nine Negro labor delegates, the first to take part in the deliberations of a nation-wide labor assembly. They represented Negro unions of caulkers, molders, painters and engineers, and five were sent by the United Laborers and Hod Carriers' Association of Philadelphia. The Negroes were seated without objection, the two leading Southern delegates, General West of Mississippi and Hal T. Walker of Alabama, voting for them. Something of the importance of the event and of the completely new departure in the practice of the labor movement is transmitted by the correspondent of the New York *Times:*

When a native Mississippian and an ex-Confederate officer, in addressing a convention refers to a colored delegate who has preceded him, as "the gentleman from Georgia," when a native Alabamian, who has for the first time crossed the Mason and Dixon line, and who was from boyhood taught to regard the Negro simply as a chattel, sits in deliberate consultation at the committee board with another delegate whose ebony face glistens with African sheen, and signs the report of the committee underneath the signature of his colored co-delegate; when an ardent and avowed Democratic partisan (from New York at that) declares with a "rich Irish brogue" that he asks for himself no privilege as a mechanic or as a citizen that he is not willing to concede to every other man, white or black—when, I say, these things can be seen and heard at a national convention, called for any purpose, then one may indeed be warranted in asserting that time works curious changes....[13]

Isaac Meyers, outstanding Negro labor leader of the period and delegate of the Colored Caulkers' Trade Union of Baltimore, told the Congress:

Silent, but powerful and far-reaching is the revolution inaugurated by your act in taking the colored laborer by the hand and telling him that his interest is common with yours.... Slavery, or slave labor, the main cause of the degradation of white labor, is no more. And it is the proud boast of my life that the slave himself had a share in striking off the one end of the fetters that bound him by the ankle, and the other end that bound you by the neck.

He posed the principal demand of the Negro worker as an equal opportunity to labor under conditions similar to those of the white workers and assured the Congress of the coöperation of Negro labor. If this coöperation was not always forthcoming in the past, he pointed out, it was because the workshops had been closed to the Negro and he had been forced to "put his labor on the market" for whatever he could get. While expressing some doubt as to how far the action of the Congress would influence local unions, Meyers declared: "We mean in all sincerity a hearty coöperation. You cannot doubt us. Where we have had the chance, we have always demonstrated it. We carry no prejudice. We are willing to let the dead past bury its dead." Finally, he urged the Congress to make a positive statement on the union of white and Negro labor. The speech was printed in full in the *Workingman's Advocate,* the organ of the National Labor Union and the most influential labor paper of the time, which also devoted considerable attention to the advance made by this Congress on the question of Negro labor.

As a result of the frank discussion and the participation of Negro delegates the Congress made a distinct advance over previous sessions. A resolution on the Negro labor question stated that "the National Labor Union knows no North, no South, no East, no West, neither color nor sex on the question of the rights of labor, and urges our colored fellow members to form organizations in all legitimate ways, and send their delegates from every State in the Union to the next Congress." For the first time definite steps were taken towards organization of Negro workers. A special committee was appointed to help organize Negro workers in Pennsylvania.

The Labor Party and Negro Labor

At the "swan" convention of the National Labor Union in 1870, where steps were taken for the organization of a Labor Reform Party, a heated debate developed on granting the privileges of the floor to J. F. Langston, Negro Reconstruction leader and Republican officeholder. This debate deserves close attention because it hinged about the relationship of the Negro and of the organized labor movement to the political parties.

The objection to the admission of Langston grew out of his efforts at the recent initial congress of the Colored National Labor Union (discussed later) to commit the Negro organization to the Republican Party. Opposition to Langston's participation was led by Alexander Troup, of the Typographers' Union and the Boston Workingmen's Assembly, and Samuel P. Cummings, delegate of the Knights of St. Crispin, the shoeworkers' union of 50,000 members and the largest labor organization in the country. Both Troup and Cummings were leaders of the Labor Party movement and of the New England Labor Reform League which ran candidates in opposition to the two major parties. Neither could be accused of objecting to Langston because he was a Negro. They had urged the participation of Negro unions in the National Labor Union. Troup had spoken together with A. A. Bradley, Negro Senator of Georgia, at a meeting held in New York to elect delegates to the Negro labor Congress, and had aided the organization of Negro workers. Cummings proudly called himself an "original Abolitionist" and had been present as a delegate of the National Labor Union at the Congress of the Colored National Labor Union where he urged unity between the two. Negro labor delegates were seated at the Congress without objections and two served on the Committee on Platform.

When the motion to admit Langston was submitted Troup objected to him because he had done his best to rope the Negro labor Congress into the Republican Party and had insulted Cummings and the other white labor delegates when they objected to "that gross piece of impertinence" which would make the Negro labor Congress "a tail to the Republican Party's kite." He was greeted with applause when he stated that "this Congress could recognize no party interest, whether it be Republican or Democratic." Cummings made it clear that he was not opposed to Langston on personal grounds. An attempt was being made, he said, to foist Langston on the Congress after he had not only done all he could to estrange the Negro from the white workers at the recent Negro labor Congress, but had also insulted him and other delegates from Massachusetts, including Negroes, because they objected. Another delegate declared that, like Cummings, he objected to no man on personal grounds, or on account of color; "no, not even to John Chinaman" (applause), but "they must all come here recognizing the great principles of the Labor Congress." He opposed Langston because he regarded him as an enemy of the Negro. Another speaker caused a sensation when he accused the opponents to Langston of prejudice and was greeted with cries of "No, No!" from the general assembly. Josiah Weare, Negro labor delegate, recalled that Langston had been sharply rebuked for his remarks by the chairman of the Negro Congress. The floor was finally denied Langston by a vote of 49 to 23. Cummings, supported by Troup, then moved for the admission of P. B. S. Pinchback, the Negro Reconstruction leader of Louisiana, but the motion was tabled. Charles H. Wesley, in his history of Negro labor, agrees that the exclusion of Langston was based on political grounds.[14]

The discussion indicated that the question of political action already was a major point of difference between the white and Negro delegates. This disagreement came sharply to the fore when Cummings introduced the resolution for the organization of a political convention composed of labor delegates from each state to form a National Labor Reform Party. Opposition to the proposal came from two sources. A number of "pure" trade unionists objected that the Congress, as a trade union gathering, should have nothing to do with politics. Opposition was also strong from the Negro delegates who were Republicans.

Isaac Meyers' speech reveals clearly the position of Negro labor with regard to independent political action. He declared that he had come to the Congress in the interest of the men who work to learn how they could best improve their economic conditions. In proportion that this was done, he believed, it would have a tendency to wipe out the prejudices which keep the Negroes from the workshops of the country. He was disappointed because the Congress had thus far devoted most of its attention to political questions. He wanted to act in complete harmony with the Congress on matters pertaining to labor's welfare and pointed out that he had signed the platform of the National Labor Union under a protest against its money reform plank. He was willing to overlook minor differences for the sake of larger unity, but he would be untrue to himself if he did not register a solemn protest against the political resolution under discussion.

The establishment of a third national political party under present conditions, he continued, would not advance the interests of the working class. The Democratic Party was the foe of labor, a power which wishes to enslave labor, while the Republican Party was the friend of labor, a power that wants to make it perpetually free. If the Republican Party is defeated a dangerous blow will be struck at the labor reform movement. "While the Republican Party is not the beau ideal of our notion of a party," he explained, "the interests of workingmen demand that they shall not hazard its success either by the organization of a new party or by an affiliation with the Democratic Party." Legislation to advance the interests of the working people could be obtained through the Republican Party, and the Congress should seek political affiliation with the Republicans.

As was to be expected, Meyers' speech was not well received. The resolution for a Labor Party was carried by a vote of 60 to 5, a number of the Negro delegates voting for the resolution. The platform adopted by the Congress pointed out "that inasmuch as both the present political parties are dominated by the non-producing classes, the highest interest of our colored fellow-citizens is with the workingmen, who, like themselves, are slaves of capital and politicians." The commitment of the Congress to the Labor Party was largely responsible for the action taken by the next national Negro labor Congress which proclaimed its separation from the National Labor Union and its allegiance to the Republican Party.[15]

Negro labor did not cut itself loose from the Republican Party because at that time it best represented the interests of the Negro people in Reconstruction. Adherence to the Republicans was the political expression of the alliance of the Negro people with the bourgeoisie in the transformation of the South. The working class, even as represented in the advanced National Labor Union, did not prove politically mature enough to write upon its own banner the democratic demands of the Negroes. It was too much to expect, as did Cummings and other advocates of independent labor politics, that the Negro workers would support a Labor Party which did not at the same time incorporate in its program the most pertinent demands of the Negro masses, such as the protection of civil rights and equal opportunity to work at equal wages. Negro labor would not abandon the party which had won its faith precisely because that party had fought for their rights, nor would they align themselves with a Labor Party which did not fully recognize the special demands of the Negro.

Labor leaders like Meyers looked with distrust upon the third party because they feared that it might imperil the victory of the Republicans and thereby the gains already made by the Negro people. The adherence of the National Labor Union to money reform was an additional cause for mistrust. The Democratic Party was winning the support of the mid-West farmers on a similar plank and in 1868 it was even suggested in labor circles that Sylvis run as second-mate on a labor presidential ticket with George A. Pendleton or General Samuel F. Cary, leading Democrats of Ohio and money reform men. There were strong elements of an alliance present between the workers and the farmers, but upon a political program which might threaten the domination of the Negro-Republican coalition over the South.

Sylvis on Reconstruction

RECONSTRUCTION policies received only passing attention in the Congresses of the National Labor Union. The only action taken was to urge the speedy restoration of the Southern states. Even a leader of the high caliber of Sylvis, although rejoicing in the results of the Civil War and urging unity between white and Negro labor, took a position on Reconstruction which was not far different from Lincoln's or Johnson's. In speeches at workers' meetings in Birmingham and Sunbury, Pennsylvania (September 1868), where he urged the formation of a Labor Reform Party, Sylvis took a very simple view of Reconstruction. The Southern states attempted to secede, he said, the North went to war to prevent them from seceding, the secessionists were whipped, and now they should be restored immediately under the Constitution, with financial aid to help overcome their economic exhaustion. He favored the immediate repeal of the Freedmen's Bureau law which "grants from $12,000,000 to $50,000,000 annually to feed and clothe the labor of one section, while the workingmen and women of another section are starving." The workers, he said, expected that the military establishment would be reduced. They "want those who are held under charge of treason to have a speedy trial, and, if found guilty, to be hung without further humbug or expense to the people." This was a laudable sentiment; but his general plan of Reconstruction was hardly such as to find favor with the Negro masses.[16]

At the beginning of 1869, Sylvis and Trevellick undertook a tour of propaganda and organization for the National Labor Union in the South. They spent two months in the South, speaking at big mass meetings in the leading cities, and succeeded in organizing a number of locals of the Molders' Union and committees of the National Labor Union. From his letters to the *Workingman's Advocate* it is clear that the trip developed no sympathy in Sylvis for the Reconstruction policy of the Republicans. He referred to Washington as "that sink of national iniquity" and to Congress as "the assembled swindlers of the nation." The Freedmen's Bureau was still a "huge swindle upon the honest workingmen of the country."

He showed, however, a surprisingly clear conception of the need for winning the Negroes to the labor program. He was very enthusiastic about a meeting of the National Labor Union in Wilmington, North Carolina, where a number of Negroes expressed support for the labor organization and pledged to organize the Negro workers in the Union. "If we can succeed in convincing these people," Sylvis wrote, "that it is in their interest to make common cause with us in these great national questions, we will have a power in this part of the country that will shake Wall Street out of its boots." As he penetrated deeper into the South he was convinced that "careful management, and a vigorous campaign, will unite the whole laboring population of the South, white and black, upon our platform." [17]

Sylvis died shortly after his tour, and the National Labor Union did not live long enough to pursue any energetic campaigns in the South.

The National Labor Union reached a high level in the development of an independent working class policy, which was undermined by agrarian greenbackism. Its collapse was in no little measure also caused by failure to grasp the revolutionary significance of Reconstruction in the South and to utilize the full possibilities it offered for an alliance with the Negro people and the middle classes.

The Colored National Labor Union

A COMBINATION of factors, such as have been discussed, tended to throw Negro labor back upon its own resources and merge into the general activities of the Negro people. The organization of Negro workers into bona fide trade unions and the development of class consciousness would have to depend largely upon the direct aid of the more matured and experienced general labor movement, particularly upon the white workers' lifting the discriminatory practices which barred Negroes from the existing unions. Nevertheless, the struggles of the Negro workers and their advances in independent organization at this early period showed the remarkable energizing effects of the democratic revolution.

A number of Negro labor organizations existed in the North and in the border cities before the Civil War. Their main activities were directed towards finding employment for Negro mechanics, education and industrial training. With the war over, the number of similar bodies increased and they tended more and more to concentrate on the regular function of trade unions. But in the South, Negro labor conventions and organizations were concerned primarily with the problems of the agricultural laborers and with the broader aspects of the democratic revolution. At the same time, however, there developed independent working class activity and organization corresponding to the undeveloped state of the proletariat.

A Southern newspaper reported indignantly in July 1865 that Negro washwomen at Jackson, Mississippi, had organized themselves into a protective association and set "exorbitant" prices for washing.[18] Discharged Negro soldiers employed at the iron works in Elyton, Alabama (Elyton became Birmingham in 1873), were driven out of town in August 1866 when they went on strike.[19] At Mobile, early in 1867, a strike of Negro workers on the levee for an advance of 25 cents an hour, spread to the sawmills and other smaller industries. The strike lasted for almost two weeks and was marked by mass demonstrations against white strikebreakers, the release of a strike leader after a demonstration in front of the city prison, and a concerted move to release fellow workers who had been placed on the chain gang.[20] In Savannah, Georgia, the dock workers, practically all Negroes, won a strike directed against the action of the City Council in imposing a poll tax of $10 on all persons employed on the wharves. The *National Workman,* organ of the Workingmen's Assembly of New York, heartily congratulated the Savannah workers on their victory and remarked:

This is not the first time since their Emancipation that they have resolutely asserted and vindicated their rights. The fact is the black man likes to be paid for his work just as well as the white man, and are rapidly learning how to secure their demands.[21]

Other strikes occurred in the iron foundries of Virginia; on the New Orleans docks for an increase in wages to $4 a day; and among the molders in Savannah against a reduction in wages. In the South, the Negro workers played a more aggressive rôle in the organization of unions than the whites. For example, a correspondent reported to the *Workingman's Advocate* a march of nearly 2,000 workers in Nashville, Tennessee, for the organization of the National Labor Union. There were no more than five white workers among the marchers. "Strange as it may seem," continued the correspondent, "our colored citizens are more active in the cause than the whites, and exhibit far more independence of capital and party influence. ...We are leaving no stone unturned in getting our workingmen together on the premises." [22]

Under the influence of the resurgent labor movement steps were taken to unite the existing Negro organizations. In 1869 the first state-wide convention of Negro labor took place at Baltimore. Delegates were elected to the forthcoming Congress of the National Labor Union. At the same time a call was issued for a national Negro labor convention to be held in Washington in December 1869. One of the signers of the call was Isaac Meyers. He was also a delegate to the next Congress of the National Labor Union where he stated that Negro labor did not wish to organize separately but was forced to do so because of their exclusion from existing trade unions. He invited the white delegates to send representatives to the Negro convention. In his speech before the Baltimore state convention,

Meyers struck the same note. The object of the national Negro convention, declared the call, was to

consolidate the colored workingmen of the several states to act in coöperation with our white fellow workingmen in every state and territory of the Union, who are opposed to distinction in the apprenticeship laws on account of color, and to so act coöperatively until the necessity for separate organization shall be deemed unnecessary.[23]

On the eve of the Washington Congress, we find the *Workingman's Advocate* in a "word of advice to the colored labor convention" warning the Negro labor delegates against political charlatans who would attempt to guide their counsels. It urged them to "act and think for themselves—independent of party dictation—if they desire and expect the support of their white fellow toilers" and stated that the National Labor Union is in earnest in its offer to help and coöperate with Negro labor.[24] The labor paper might have been more effective in its appeal to the Negro workers if it had at the same time devoted its attention to removing the restrictions which barred Negro labor from the white trade unions. The young Negro labor movement was concerned primarily with winning equal opportunity for Negro workers. Until discriminatory obstacles were removed it would be impossible for Negro labor, unembarrassed by other considerations, to participate in the activities of the labor movement as a whole.

When the Colored National Labor Convention met at Washington it was evident that the issues of Reconstruction would play an important part in its proceedings. Of the 203 delegates, 54 came from the states of the deep South. But only nine of the Southern delegates were workers; there were nine farmers, 28 lawyers, preachers, teachers and merchants, and eight

whose occupation was not given. The occupations of
the Northern and border delegates are not known, but
it is evident from the proceedings that the majority
were professional people. Negro unions sent delegates,
but as a whole it was a labor convention only in name
and its decisions on the labor question were shaped by
the contingencies of Reconstruction.

The Langston incident, which, as we have seen, was
so sharply recalled at the 1870 Congress of the National
Labor Union, arose around the question of admitting
McLane, president of the National Plasterers' Union.
Langston vigorously opposed his admission as a delegate, declaring that McLane held allegiance to the
Labor Party. If he were permitted to speak in the name
of a party "which sought to build itself on the ruins of
the Democratic and Republican parties," Langston
held, the Convention would be dangerously committed
and might prejudice the aid of the Republican Party.

The attitude of Langston was not shared by all the
Negro labor delegates. George T. Downing of Rhode
Island, who was acting chairman, sharply rebuked
Langston for his speech, ordered the admission of
McLane and appealed to the white workers for unity
in a common cause. He recognized the part played by
the Republican Party in overthrowing slavery and
conceded it "respect and support in view of its agency
in freeing us from that degradation." But his support
was not unstinted: "We think that it should have been
more consistent, more positive in its dealings with our
and the country's enemies; ... We should be secured
in the soil, which we have enriched in our toil and
blood, and to which we have a double entitlement."
Meyers and Sella Martin, of Massachusetts, also criticized Langston and appealed to the white and black
workers to work harmoniously together in the cause of
labor.

Discussion revolved principally around questions of land and equal rights. The Southern delegates especially persisted in raising the demand for land. Rainey of South Carolina said that the convention would not meet the expectations of the Negro people unless it took steps for the distribution of the land "so that they would not be obliged to build up another Southern aristocracy." Another delegate suggested that the convention appeal to Congress to distribute government-owned land "as it had failed to enact laws to confiscate the rebel lands for this purpose." Hamilton of Florida attacked the land monopoly in the South and told the convention that the landowners not only refused to sell a foot of land to Negroes at any price but also refused to sell implements or farm animals to the freedmen. The South Carolina delegation reported that the average wage of agricultural laborers in the South was $60 a year and pointed out that there was sufficient free land in the South to supply each freedmen with 40 acres.

The convention finally adopted a memorial to Congress asking that $2,000,000 be appropriated to purchase land and sell it at cost to the freedmen, who would be required to pay it out in five years. Other resolutions objected to large land grants to railroads and corporations, urged that these lands be given to the Negroes, and recommended the creation of a permanent government bureau for the purpose of obtaining homesteads.

A high degree of internationalism was shown in a resolution of sympathy for the Cubans which pledged support to their struggle for independence from Spanish rule. Sella Martin was designated as a delegate to the International Labor Congress in Paris the following September.

In the Platform of the Colored National Labor Union

principal emphasis was placed upon democratic rights, the most pressing and immediate need of the Negro people. At the head was the demand for a national system of public education with equal opportunities for Negroes. Equality in industry was raised as the key need of the Negro workers and a protest was registered against discrimination by the trade unions. Free immigration for all nationalities was endorsed but the importation of coolie labor was deprecated as "slavery in a new form." Negroes were urged to form coöperative associations in industry and on the land "as a remedy against the exclusion of our people from other workshops on account of color, as a means of furnishing employment, as well as protection against the aggression of capital and as the easiest and shortest method for enabling every man to procure a homestead for his family." Capital, the Platform said, is not an enemy of labor. "The great conflict daily waged between them is for want of a better understanding." Negro workers were urged, however, to form associations in every state and to communicate with the Bureau of Labor, established by the convention, so "that justice may be meted out to them as though they lived in the large cities."

No clear program of organization along trade union lines was advanced in the Prospectus of the Bureau of Labor, issued in February 1870. Each worker was advised to try to become a capitalist or at least assure himself a homestead. Negro workers were urged to organize for the purpose of bettering their conditions, but they were warned that "mixed organizations have always proven disastrous to the labor reform movement, except in delegated bodies." Little is said as to the form of organization and emphasis is again placed upon coöperatives.[25]

The Colored National Labor Union was neither a

trade union body nor a political class organization.
The Platform exhibits great confusion on the labor
question and reflects the urgency of the democratic
needs of the people. The convention was really a Negro
people's assembly and the organization created by it
can be characterized as a broad Negro congress encom-
passing the pressing needs of all strata of the people.
But it was the first Negro congress in which labor was
represented as such and exerted some independent
influence. As a whole, its significance rests in the fact
that it was the first national organization of the Negro
people in the new period.

The labor movement welcomed the new organization. Cummings, Trevellick and other leading labor
leaders were present at the convention as delegates
of the National Labor Union. In his account of the
proceedings in the labor press, Cummings regretted
the Langston incident as showing a tendency to separation and said that he would have been better satisfied if the convention had decided to join the Labor
Party movement. "But," he said, "fresh as they are
from slavery, looking as they naturally do upon the
Republican Party as their deliverers from bondage, it
is not strange that they hesitate about joining any
other movement." [26]

In an editorial, the *Workingman's Advocate* hailed
the "grand inaugural movement ... to consolidate the
colored element of the Southern states which can
ultimately have but one result—a clear alliance with,
and an endorsement of the principles of the National
Labor Union." It deplored the effort of the Republicans to control the convention "although the results
cannot have afforded them much consolation." The
journal would have "preferred that the voice of labor
should have been heard a little more distinctly," but

it pronounced itself, upon the whole, satisfied with the results.[27]

As it became more and more an appendage of the Republican Party, the Colored National Labor Union disintegrated quickly. Attempts at organization along trade union lines were made, especially by the labor leaders. Isaac Meyers, who had been elected president of the organization, undertook a tour of some Southern states. At Norfolk, Virginia, he addressed a large labor meeting where he declared that the time was past "for the establishment of organizations based upon color." He opposed the tendency toward separate organization as expressed in the convention and in the Prospectus and urged white and Negro workers in the same trade to organize together wherever possible. Other meetings were held where emphasis was placed upon the formation of coöperative societies.[28]

The second convention took place in January 1871. Delegates from only ten states were present—an indication that the Labor Union was not taking root. In his opening address, Meyers again opposed separate organization and urged coöperation between white and black labor. But the resolutions of the body did not show any advance over the previous convention, beyond designating delegates in the Southern states to organize labor unions. The election of Frederick Douglass as president and other non-labor elements to the national offices, as well as a declaration of allegiance to the Republican Party, marked the complete subordination of the N.C.L.U. to the Republicans. The third convention, held at Columbia, South Carolina, in October 1871, was practically a Negro Republican convention, which raised the democratic demands of the people.

In April 1872 the final gathering met as a Southern States' Convention in New Orleans to consolidate

Negro support for the Republicans in the presidential election. Labor leaders such as Meyers had practically disappeared from the leadership. Frederick Douglass and other prominent Republicans dominated the sessions. The gathering issued a platform which praised the administration of Grant, acknowledged indebtedness to Charles Sumner, "the Gibraltar of our cause and the north star of our hopes," asked for protection of Negroes in their rights, pledged support to the Radical Republicans and repudiated "any sympathy or connection" with the Labor Reform Convention which had recently taken place at Columbus, Ohio.[29] The final demise of the Colored National Labor Union was marked by an editorial in the issue of May 17, 1874, of *The New National Era*, of which Frederick Douglass was editor, entitled "The Folly, Tyranny and Wickedness of Labor Unions." [30]

State Negro labor conventions were held in 1870 and 1871 in Tennessee, Texas, Alabama, Missouri and Georgia, on the call of the state officers of the national organization. In character they were general people's congresses and no permanent state labor organizations resulted. They showed the independent activities of the Negro people in fighting for radical Reconstruction and equal rights but did not signify any important advance in the development of an independent labor movement in the South. However, a number of local trade unions were formed among the Negro workers, which carried on successful strike struggles, particularly among the longshoremen of Baltimore and Charleston.

The influence of the Republicans among the Negro workers did not go unchallenged by the advanced labor movement. The *Workingman's Advocate* continued an editorial campaign against the efforts of both Parties to win Negro support. It asked the white workers "whether it is either politic or right that the party of all parties most deeply interested in securing their [the Negroes'] influence should stand listless and indifferent at this important juncture." With prophetic vision, the *Advocate* vigorously pronounced its belief that the "success of the labor movement for years to come, depends upon the coöperation and support of the colored race, and further, that it will be only through the grossest culpability and mismanagement that they can be driven into the ranks of their oppressors. *Their interests are our interests; our interests are theirs.*" It pointed out that the capitalists attempted to antagonize the white and Negro workers "to secure a new lease of power, while the victims of both shades will be ground to powder between the upper and nether millstones." The workers' paper called for a stubborn struggle against "unholy prejudice" and urged labor to follow up consistently the example set at the National Labor Union Congresses in admitting Negro delegates.[31]

Editorials such as these, as well as direct organizational and political appeals to the Negro to participate in national and local labor parties, show that while white labor was willing to unite with black it had not yet learned how to raise those specific issues in which the Negro workers were most interested.

The First International

THE furthest advance in understanding the urgency of the Negro question and its import to the labor movement as a whole was made by the early Socialist groups and sections of the First International. Modern Socialism in the United States found its start in the Civil War decade. The forerunners were organizations of German émigrés such as the Communist Club of

New York and the General German Labor Association. In the upsurge of the labor movement after the war, the German workers, who held a strategic position as skilled craftsmen, played a leading rôle. They also laid the foundation in this country of scientific socialism. In the late 'sixties the German Socialist groups organized the American sections of the International Workingman's Association (the First International).

German workers' groups had played a prominent part in the struggle against slavery. Many of their members enlisted in the Northern army and a number led regiments which they themselves recruited. The Communist Club especially was active in the Abolition movement, some of its members even joining the Radical wing of the Republican Party. Other revolutionary German émigrés settled in the South where they carried on an energetic campaign against slavery. Hermann Meyer, a close friend of Weydemeyer and later a member of the I.W.A., went to Montgomery, Alabama, in 1859, where he carried on agitation against slavery until he was forced to flee the State. Adolph Douai, who became a prominent Socialist editor, founded the *San Antonio* (Texas) *Zeitung* in the early 'fifties and carried on Abolitionist propaganda. His life was threatened on a number of occasions but he persisted in his publishing activity, setting up the type and printing the paper himself. After three years he was finally forced to leave. The Negroes did not forget. In 1866, Douai, who was then in New York, received a newspaper from San Antonio which carried the following notice in large type on the front page:

"This paper, owned and printed by Negroes, is printed on the same press on which Dr. Douai first fought in Texas for Negro Emancipation. Let the gratitude of the colored race to him be expressed in this, that they remember his efforts for their freedom."

These advanced German workers combined their agitation for an independent political party of the working class with demands for Negro rights. The first political party of the workers based on Socialist ideas was the Social Party of New York and Vicinity, formed by the amalgamation of the Communist Club and the General German Labor Association. In its platform, presented at a mass meeting in New York on January 20, 1868, two planks having direct bearing upon the Negro were included. One demanded the repeal of all discriminatory laws and the other favored the eligibility of all citizens of the United States for office. This was the first time in the new period a working class organization raised the question of equal rights. The party was soon dissolved in favor of the Labor Reform Party announced by the National Labor Union.

Section 1 of New York was the most active body of the First International in the United States. The Section was also affiliated to the National Labor Union as Labor Union No. 5. It formed a link between the national organization of American labor and the international labor movement. Its activities with regard to the Negro reveal a clear consciousness of the rôle demanded of the white workers in establishing solidarity between white and black labor. In a report to President Trevellick of the National Labor Union by F. A. Sorge, the outstanding early Socialist leader, it was stated that Labor Union No. 5 was endeavoring to spread the movement among the labor organizations of the Negroes and other nationalities in New York.

This was no idle boast, judging from even passing reference to the work of the Section in available sources. In October 1869, Section 1 appointed a committee to found trade unions among the Negro workers. Results were quick, for only two weeks later a delegation of Negro workers appeared before the Section to thank them for their coöperation and to report that a trade union of 90 members had already been formed. On this occasion, A. A. Bradley, Negro Senator from Georgia, addressed the gathering. The following February, when the Negro union was unable to obtain a hall, the Section provided one. Next month, Section 1 gained the admittance of the Negro labor unions of the city to the Workingmen's Union, the central city labor body.

The activities of the Internationals among the Negro workers led to their participation in the great eight-hour movement in New York City. On September 13, 1871, 20,000 workers marched in the eight-hour parade, called by the Workingmen's Union, which inaugurated extensive strikes in the city for the shorter workday. Negro members of a waiters' union and Negro plasterers from Brooklyn marched with the I.W.A. sections. The red flag carried by the Internationals and inscribed with the slogan, "Workingmen of All Countries Unite!" was the first to be carried through the streets of New York. They were greeted along the line of march with cries of *"Vive la Commune!"* When the procession reached City Hall, where 5,000 awaited it, the Negro section was greeted with applause.[32] This was a great advance. Only a few years before race riots had taken place on the docks when the employers attempted to break a strike of Irish longshoremen by importing Negro dock workers from the border cities.

Shortly after, on December 18, 1871, a company of Negro militia, the Skidmore Guard, participated in a demonstration called by the Internationals to protest the execution of three leading Parisian Communards. A similar demonstration the week before had been broken up by the police. Over 10,000 of all colors and nationalities were in the line of march. The Negroes could hardly have participated in actions such as the Commune demonstration and the eight-hour parade unless their friendship had already been won in day-to-day activities and common efforts in the labor movement.

"Such is progress," declared the *Workingman's Advocate,* referring to the participation of Negro plasterers in the eight-hour strike and to a meeting of the New York I.W.A. which cheered enthusiastically an invitation to participate in a celebration of Negro workers.[33]

Similar activities were carried on by the I.W.A. sections in other cities. In Chicago, members of the I.W.A. played a leading rôle in the Labor Reform League of Cook County, which carried on political activities among the Negro population. Richard Hinton, who had taken part in John Brown's uprising at Harper's Ferry, was among the most active members of the Washington Section. In 1875, the Labor Party of Illinois led a demonstration for relief of the unemployed in Chicago and presented demands to the Mayor which included provisions against discrimination on account of color.

In May 1872, Frederick Douglass was nominated as Vice-President with Victoria Woodhull, the women's rights leader, as President on a national ticket at a convention called by a split-off section of the I.W.A., the "renegade Prince Street Council." The program evolved at the convention included only one labor demand, the legal eight-hour day, and raised to the forefront demands such as women's suffrage, criminal reform, and the creation of a merchant marine. The sections of the I.W.A. which participated in the convention withdrew because of the bourgeois reform nature of the program and the "general humbug" of the gathering. The ticket was not run in the elections.[34]

The tradition of solidarity between white and Negro labor was established early in the organized labor movement. The National Labor Union, and particularly the small but effective Socialist movement, made noteworthy advances in this direction. But forces which disintegrated the energetic labor movement of the 'sixties and early 'seventies intervened. By the time the labor movement was again to revive, a new relationship of class forces already existed in the country.

CHAPTER VII

REVOLUTION AND
COUNTER-REVOLUTION

"White Superiority" as a Political Program

THE strategy of counter-revolution in the South was to split the Radical Republican coalition. There were two phases in the development of this strategy. On the one hand, an attempt was made to separate the Negroes and native white Republicans from "carpetbag" leadership and ally them with the old Confederate leaders in the Democratic Party. When this proved unsuccessful the principal emphasis was shifted to the "race issue"; "white superiority" as a political program emerged hand in hand with increased terroristic activity against Negro and white Republicans.

Birth in the North, if we are to believe Bourbon publicists, endowed a person with a natural aptitude for venality, corruption, barbarism and all the evils a human may possibly possess. In the language of the more raucous editors, Northern Republicans who were active in Southern politics were "long-haired Barbarians" and "nigger-worshippers," than which, it seems, there can be no greater crime in the South. The more moderate editors told their readers that Radicals were strangers and foreigners in their midst who had come to dissever the sympathies of the Negroes from their old masters with whom their highest interests were naturally and indissolubly linked. And it is surprising to find how many scholarly historians of our present day and age believe them.

The carpetbagger as pictured for us by many historians in colors stolen from the Bourbon press is largely a myth. Most carpetbaggers were soldiers or officers in the Union Army who remained in the South when they were discharged from the service. Ficklen, the historian of Reconstruction in Louisiana, estimates that between five and ten thousand remained in the state in 1866. Many were sincere Abolitionists who had taken up weapons to fight for their cause and then remained to take part in the transformation of the South. Undoubtedly, some took advantage of the economic opportunities, bought up auctioned land and speculated, and others became large planters. Among them were people who, in the spirit of the times, were friendly to the railroad lobbies and did not refuse easy graft. But generally they were advanced bourgeois progressives in politics. Judge Tourgee, a Supreme Court Justice of North Carolina, did not shrink from the label of carpetbagger, putting Columbus, the Pilgrims and Jesus Christ in the same category. If the Bourbons directed so much of both their verbal and gun fire against the "carpetbaggers," it was because they were among the ablest organizers and leaders of Reconstruction.

The dominant section of the Bourbon Democrats during the years 1867-1868 adopted a paternal and conciliatory attitude towards the Negroes, appealing to them to join the Democratic Party ranks. The *Richmond Examiner,* for example, declared in 1867 that "the Southern people desire to see a fair trial of the Negro's capacity for self-government, and, most assuredly, every interest of the South urges her to desire also a successful issue of the experiment." It even conceded the possibility that the Negroes might yet prove to be "industrious, intelligent and upright citizens." [1] General Wade Hampton, former Confederate officer, large landowner and later the first governor of South

Carolina under the counter-revolutionary régime, addressed a large meeting of Negroes in Columbia, speaking from the same platform as Beverly Nash, and told them that the destinies of the old leaders and of the Negroes were dependent upon each other. Even Benjamin H. Hill, the stalwart reactionary of Georgia, came to agree with Hampton that the wisest thing was to concede political rights to Negroes and use this support against the Republicans.

This sudden discovery of common interest with the Negroes on the part of the old masters was a political strategy. Overnight they professed conversion to the principles of the Negro-rights Amendments and appealed to the former slaves for support against "usurpers" from the North. The Negroes were invited to Democratic Party conventions and political rallies. In Alabama, for instance, they were urged to attend a conservative convention in 1867 to satisfy themselves "that the whites of the South" intend that the freedmen "shall remain free and possess their rights for all time." The Negroes were warned against "separating themselves from the old citizens" by their political activities in the Union Leagues and "earnestly informed" that they and the planters must tread the same onward path. "Let every white man and honest black man in the State," counseled the *Montgomery Weekly Advertiser,* "fall into the Democratic ranks and make a crushing charge upon the shattered cohorts of scalawags and carpetbaggers." [2] Another Democratic paper called upon all colored men to assist in rescuing the "native State from the pillage and ruinous rule of adventurous office seeking exotics." [3] The Bourbon press gave prominent play to statements and letters from a few Negro Copperheads and Uncle Toms, treating them in a most respectful manner. Negro Democrats were always "intelligent citizens" while Negro

Republicans were "niggers," uneducated and uncouth.

Editors who had abused the Republicans in the most insulting terms for meeting with Negroes in political conventions, now invited the Negroes to attend Democratic gatherings, offered to sit and consult with them. They must have ardently believed their own propaganda about the idiocy of the Negro to think that he would ever trust his former master or the old Confederate leaders. This policy proved to be a universal failure because it was based on the supposition that the Negro masses were a blind following ready to submit to any leaders.

The Bourbons soon discovered that they could never win the Negro people. They then transferred their affections to the poor white population and the small farmers and based their politics upon the program of "white superiority." The Richmond *Enquirer and Examiner*, for example, learned at the very first election in which Negroes participated that they were arrayed "in solid phalanx against the interests, nay the property, and even the lives" of the planters and took this as "the most irrefragable proof that their hostility to us is instinctive and ineradicable. Nothing, therefore, remains for us to do but to meet the issue they have thus thrust upon us and defend ourselves like men." [4]

An editorial in the *Independent Monitor*, entitled "Awake! Arise!" is representative of the popular terminology of the counter-revolutionary program. "Let every man at the South," it calls, "through whose veins the unalloyed Caucasian blood courses, who is not a vile adventurer or carpetbagger, forthwith align himself in the rapidly increasing ranks of his species, so that we may the sooner overwhelmingly crush, with one mighty blow, the preposterous wicked dogma of Negro equality!" Then follow verbose pæans to "white supremacy" and fulminations against "Negro barbarism," culminating in the cry: "We must render this either a white man's government, or convert the land into a Negro man's cemetery." [5] The same paper openly advocated the formation of the K.K.K. in each community "whose peculiar service should be the condign cleansing of neighborhoods of all human impurities." To make the meaning clearer, the editor explained: "If to every tree in our forest-like streets were attached a rope; and to the ends of each rope a Northern and Southern Radical, gathered from the Loyal League assembled in our courthouse, then might we once more live in peace and harmony." [6]

To the accompaniment of such tunes, sometimes more subtle sometimes harsher, the counter-revolution ushered in its extra-legal armed bands of K.K.K. and similar organizations.* Essentially, these bands constituted a guerrilla army, functioning more or less secretly, whose main duties were to terrorize the whites who followed the Republicans, intimidate the local Radical Republican leaders and prevent the Negroes from exercising their political rights. One Republican newspaper warned the Bourbons that no one doubts that when the former rebels organize a "white man's party" to attempt to deprive the freedmen of any of their rights they "will peril life to defend and preserve them." [7]

A sporadic, but incessant civil war raged anew in the South. In some states it terminated early, in others

---

* The Ku Klux Klan was started by a group of former officers of the Confederate army in the small town of Pulaski, Tenn., in 1865. Similar groups were soon formed in other states and were federated in May 1867. The whole organization was headed by a Grand Wizard; each state had a Grand Dragon, each county a Grand Giant and each locality a Grand Cyclops. Besides the Klan, other extra-legal, counter-revolutionary bands flourished, among them the Knights of the White Camelia in Louisiana, the White Brotherhood in North Carolina and the Knights of the Rising Sun in Texas.

it lasted until the bitter betrayal of 1876. The revolution was defeated as soon as the Negroes were isolated from their allies. Counter-revolutionary terror was an important although not a decisive factor. The Negroes fought back, but the outcome did not depend primarily upon them. The White Terror could be effective only when the original Radical Republican coalition disintegrated as a revolutionary force.

Rupture of the Radical Republican Coalition

NATIONAL developments in the early 'seventies were already creating a rift in the ranks of the Radical Republicans. Opposition to the new industrial and financial oligarchy gained momentum. Loose and hectic financing of the railroads, government aid to brokers and financiers, the hearty reception at Washington of the manufacturers' and corporation lobbies, the high tariff policy, large grants of free land to railroads and other corporations—these were the less sightly aspects of the boom development which so quickly rounded out the continent and created new industrial empires. It was a roaring decade set off by the explosion of Civil War and with rocket speed accomplishing tasks which had demanded a century in England.

Labor, as we have seen, took the field early against the new leaders of the nation. The farmers and the small property-holders revolted against the high-handed financial manipulations of the Wall Street brokers. In the presidential campaign of 1868, greenbackism already appeared prominently in the Democratic Party platform. Linked with demands for the immediate restoration of the states, general amnesty for the ex-Confederates, and regulation of suffrage by the states themselves, was the slogan which was born in Ohio: "The same currency for the bondholder and

the plough-holder." The farmers were protesting
against the high railroad rates which mulcted much of
their profits. The countryside murmured, "Cost of production plus a reasonable rate of profit"—a cry which
was soon to rise in crescendo. The Granges were organized in 1867 and were already beginning to show their
political strength in 1873 when, in coöperation with
the Democrats, they elected the governor and legislature of Wisconsin, reduced the Republican majorities
in Iowa and Minnesota, and showed strength in Illinois
and Kansas.

These new class conflicts were also having effect
upon the Radical Republican coalition. By March
1870 the Radicals had recorded in the Constitution the
last victory of the Abolition democracy in the form of
the Fifteenth Amendment, which prohibited states
from denying the right of suffrage to any citizen on
account of race, color or previous condition of servitude. They also registered positive measures in the
Enforcement Acts, which were passed in 1870 and 1871,
to suppress the K.K.K. and protect Negroes in their
rights under the three Amendments.

The Enforcement Acts were drastic and revolutionary measures. The first (May 31, 1870) penalized state
officers and any person who attempted to deprive citizens of the suffrage and their civil rights, and authorized the use of the Army to enforce these rights.
The second Act (February 28, 1871) gave Federal
officers and courts control over registration and voting in congressional elections. The Ku Klux Act of
April 20, 1871, gave the Federal government the power
to suppress conspiracies which threatened political and
civil rights, characterized such combinations as rebellion against the United States and empowered the
President to suspend the protection of Habeas Corpus
in the affected districts.

But the Radical Republicans never fully utilized these measures to suppress counter-revolution in the South. When an attempt was made to enforce the Ku Klux Act, opposition even among the Republicans was strong. In 1871 President Grant went the full limit of this Act in nine South Carolina counties. After being duly warned, the K.K.K. failed to disband or give up their arms, and United States troops were sent to South Carolina in November. Some 500 or 600 persons were arrested but only a few were convicted. Conservative Republicans, who remained cold at the outrages of the Klan, were horrified at the arrest of white planters and hoodlums by the military. Under the Enforcement Acts during 1870-1876 there were in all the Southern states only 1,208 convictions, while 2,350 cases were dismissed or quashed and 281 resulted in acquittals.[8] Most of the convictions took place in South Carolina and Mississippi where the Radical governments were the strongest. The Negroes never received any really effective military aid from their Northern ally in the struggle against armed counter-revolution. The effective provisions of the Acts were eventually repealed or declared unconstitutional.

In general, the temper of the Radical Republicans had changed. The prime obstacle to capitalist expansion had been removed with the abolition of chattel slavery. Restoration of the slave power had been effectively prevented and the financial-industrial bourgeoisie was well entrenched. The other tasks of the revolution in the South could be left to work themselves out, although it was a matter of first concern to the Radical Republicans that they maintain political hegemony. Not at the price, however, of social unrest and continued upheaval. Social peace was needed to obtain the full benefits of the new plantation production and the tremendous internal market. The re-

volt of the farmers and the workers was disquieting
enough, and peace in the rear would relieve the bourgeoisie to meet new threats. If peace could be obtained
at the price of the hard-won rights of the Negroes,
this was but a slight concession to ask of the bourgeoisie. Their hearts, after all, were with the men of
property and the "substantial citizens." If they could
patch up a settlement with these in the South, which
would assure peaceful exploitation, it would be much
more to their liking.

Conciliation became the popular note. During 1871,
Congress was liberal in pardoning former Confederate
leaders who asked for the privilege "in good faith."
A number of general amnesty bills were defeated only
by the action of Sumner in attaching as an amendment his Civil Rights Bill. It is an illuminating com-
mentary upon the changing mood of the Republicans
that while they were willing to restore full civil rights
to their former enemy they were unwilling to guarantee social privileges to their ally. When the
Amnesty Act finally did pass in May 1872, Sumner
declared: "The time has not come for amnesty. You
must be just to the colored race before you are generous
to former rebels." Coming from Sumner, who was not
opposed to amnesty in principle, this was a nice moral
plea which received its due applause but touched no
real interest of his colleagues.

The passage of the Amnesty Act marked acquiescence to the course of reaction. It removed political disabilities from leaders of the old slavocracy and
gave them *carte blanche* to political power. The Bill
reduced the number of former Confederates excluded
from office from some 150,000 to between 300 and 500.
Leading secessionists and counter-revolutionists, such
as Alexander H. Stephens, General Wade Hampton
and Benjamin H. Hill, regained their full political

rights. True, they had never been silenced or restricted in their open political activity. But now they were empowered to hold office as well.

When the Amnesty Bill was passed reaction already ruled in Virginia, Georgia and North Carolina, where a liberal use of the pardon contributed to the restoration of old rulers. Virginia was never under Radical government, thanks to the interference of General Schofield, who aligned himself with the conservatives. The first election of 1869 resulted in a Conservative Republican victory, saving the state, according to the General, "from the vile government and spoliation which cursed the other Southern states." Schofield had objected to the new State Constitution because of its severe disqualification of the old leaders and on his insistence the Constitution passed without these clauses. Under his military rule many of the former Confederates were pardoned and the local Radical Republicans were hampered in their activities. In Georgia, White Terror and the split in the Republican ranks on the race issue, led to the Democrats' winning the state legislature in 1870. The following year the Radical Republican Governor was forced to resign and flee the state. In 1872 a Democratic Governor was inaugurated.

North Carolina was thrown back into the lap of its former masters in 1870, when the President refused to send Federal troops to suppress the K.K.K. The reign of terror against Negroes and Radical Republican leaders was described by Judge Albion W. Tourgee as follows: "Of the slain there were enough to furnish forth a battlefield and all from these three classes, the Negro, the scalawag and the carpetbagger.... The wounded in this silent warfare were more thousands than those who groaned upon the slopes of Gettysburg." [9] And yet, when the Governor sent "Kirk's militia"—composed largely of white mountaineers and Negroes—to the most affected area, a tirade of criticism was directed against him from all parts of the country. The mountaineer-Negro militia did its duty by arresting a few hundred K.K.K. rowdies, but they were all freed by the courts. In the elections, the Democrats gained a large majority in the state legislature and elected five out of seven congressmen. The Republican Governor was impeached and removed from office for using the militia against the Klan.

Under the Capitol dome, revolutionary passion had cooled off considerably. Reactionary victories in the South and K.K.K. terror aroused only meek and ineffectual rejoinders. The contradictory aspects of the Radical Republican coalition were making themselves strongly felt. By 1872 a complete rupture occurred between the two principal wings of the Party, the industrial-financial oligarchy and the old middle-class Abolition democracy. The bolters from the regular Republicans included Horace Greeley, Charles Francis Adams, Lyman Trumbull, Carl Schurz, George W. Julian and Charles Sumner. These leaders had taken up the battle of the "common people" against the oligarchy, of the farmers against the railroads, of the taxpayers against the swindlers, and were also liberal in their attitude to labor. They were primarily representatives of the lower middle class in town and country, who revolted at the government frauds and extensive aid to financiers and corporations under the Grant Administration. The *Nation,* describing a mass meeting of Liberal Republicans at Cooper Institute, New York, said that "the audience was composed of that sober, thoughtful middle class, equally removed from wealth and poverty." [10] Like Johnson before them, they attempted the middle course and were thrown into the arms of the Democrats.

The bolters met in convention, drew up a platform and nominated candidates for the 1872 presidential election. Both the platform and the candidates were a negation of everything the Abolition democracy had stood for in the conflict with the slavocracy. They demanded the removal of all the political disqualifications against Southern whites, cessation of military rule in the South and—contradiction of contradictions!—suffrage and equal rights for the Negro. One was not possible without the other and here they faced their great enigma. Negro rights could not be maintained in the South without at the same time taking repressive measures against the reaction, but the reaction offered itself as a strong ally of the middle class from the Right against the bourgeois oligarchy.

Horace Greeley, the wavering Abolitionist—who, at Secession cried: "Erring Brothers, Go in Peace!" and later stood bail for Jefferson Davis—was nominated for President. There could have been no more fitting person to typify the wavering politics of the middle class at this time. The complete rout to the Right was indicated in the support of the Liberal Republican ticket by the Democratic Party in its regular convention. Middle-class opposition to the new oligarchy, unless based upon alliance with popular democracy in the South and with the working class, was bound to travel in the direction of a coalition with the extreme Right.

The renegades and the Democrats suffered a resounding defeat. Grant was reëlected by a large majority and the Radical Republicans won two-thirds of the seats in Congress. The split of 1872 was but the shadow of more ominous events ahead. The financial panic and depression of 1873 (partly caused by speculation in railroads and government bonds), revelations of Radical Republican corruption in Washington involving high administrative officers, mass unrest among the farmers and workers, and further gains of reaction in the South contributed to a reversal of the verdict of 1872. In the elections of 1874 a number of Southern states sent solid Democratic delegations to Congress. The Republicans were reduced to only one-third of the seats in the House, losing control of it for the first time since 1861. There was real danger that the Democrats, representing a coalition of the Bourbons and the middle class, might gain national control in 1876.

Split of the Party in the South

THE triple alliance which constituted the Radical Republican Party in the South not only was subject to the same disruptive influences as the national party but had to bear the brunt of the counter-revolutionary attack.

From the start, the most uncertain elements in the alliance were the small farmers of the up-lands and the small urban middle class. These were the first to break away from the Radical Republicans. Charges of corruption and fraud against the Radicals found acceptance among these strata. They were small property-holders who opposed the financial-industrial oligarchy and felt in some degree the burden of increased taxation. When the reactionaries combined appeals to property interest and race prejudice in the cry, "They are taxing you to educate Negroes in mixed schools!" they found a ready response.

Since the war a new middle class had arisen in the South. The railroads had opened interior markets and connected the inland cotton producing areas with the Southern ports. Central cotton markets sprang up in New Orleans, Savannah, Memphis, forming an outlet

for the rich interior plantation areas. The first cotton
exchanges were created in these cities only in 1870-72.
The reorganization of the plantation upon a share-
cropping and tenant basis, and an increase in small
farmholdings, led to the rapid formation of towns. The
local credit merchant, supplying tenants and share-
croppers on credit through the plantation owner, was a
new phenomenon of the Reconstruction period. The
country stores formed the nuclei for new towns and
villages. In South Carolina, for example, there were
only 16 places rated as towns in 1860, while the census
of 1880 listed 110 towns and villages and another
authority placed the number of towns and trading
centers at 493.[11] There emerged a new merchant, credit
and town business class, intimately connected with the
plantation system.*

There existed a surprisingly clear conception of the
new potential market opened up by the abolition of
the slave system. The Commissioner of Industrial
Resources of Alabama in 1869 argued against a return
to the slave system in the following manner:

> The average annual expenditure of a planter owning num-
> bers of slaves before the war was about $16 per head. The
> immediate effect of making slaves into freedmen is the
> average annual expenditure by them of not less than $100
> each. The immense aid to the business of the country re-
> sulting from the change needs not to be commented upon.[12]

And a Northern newspaper depicted the benefits
arising from public education of the Negro in terms

---

* Industry in the South developed very slowly during the
Reconstruction period. The number of spindles in the textile mills
was doubled between 1860 and 1880, but the industry still
remained a negligible factor. By 1880 the iron and steel industry
in the Birmingham area was beginning to assume sizeable proportions. Important industrial development, however, did not
take place until the 'eighties and 'nineties.

close to the heart of businessmen: The North sells to
the South

all sorts of Yankee notions amounting in the year to many
hundreds of thousands of dollars, and destined soon to
amount to many millions. The most that we Yankees have
to do to insure to our own tills the profits of this trade is
to hasten the work of education. England, at a great cost to
treasure and life, compasses sea and land with her navies
to establish a colony which will buy its goods of Manchester
and Birmingham; we, at a cost not worth mentioning, and
with a light brigade of school mistresses, can organize at
our own doors a colony—so to speak—that will be worth
more to us than any of England's most flourishing depend-
encies.[13]

The rise of a new middle class closely associated
with the plantation economy, as well as the spread of
commercial cotton production to the small farms of
the up-lands, hastened reaction in the South. The
victory of counter-revolution was anticipated in the
South also by a split in the Republican Party.
The Reform or Liberal Republicans were mostly native
whites of the middle class in town and country. They
bolted from the regular party on the issue of taxation,
aid to the railroads and financial groups, state credits
to encourage industry, exemption of new industries
from taxation, and fraud.

A number of leading Negro Reconstructionists joined
the bolters chiefly on the issue of civil reform. R. H.
Cain, a Negro leader of South Carolina, called upon
his people to oust corrupt office-holders and said that
he "would favor sending to the legislature honest
mechanics and farmers whose minds are not biased by
political chicanery; at any rate let us have honest
men who are identified with the country's prosperity
and the people's interest." [14] But the overwhelming
majority of the Negro people stuck by the Radical

Republicans, for they saw in the so-called Reform movement a strong tendency to alliance with the Bourbons and a real threat to their political and civil rights.

Even within their own party, however, the Negroes had to wage a constant struggle for office and equal rights. We have already seen how inadequately the Negroes were represented in the state governments. For the Negroes, the fight for office was not a fight for spoils. It was primarily a question of obtaining their political rights and being in a position where they could enforce them. They made it increasingly clear that they knew their political strength and did not intend to let white men hold the offices while they did the voting. In the state nominating convention of the Republican Party for the Mississippi election of 1873, for example, the Negro Republicans demanded that at least three of the seven state officers should go to them and they received the nominations for Lieutenant-Governor, Secretary of State and Superintendent of Education. The Vicksburg *Plain Dealer,* a Negro newspaper, declared that white men had always insisted on holding the offices, while the colored men did the voting, but that "this thing had played out." [15] A correspondent of a Republican paper warned against discrimination by white Republicans and said:

To suppose that the colored people do not notice these indications, these slights, these distinctions, made solely on account of color, by these men whom they have helped into position, is simply absurd.[16]

Democrats as well as dissident Republicans took advantage of this struggle for office and the dissatisfaction of Negro Republicans to turn the tide against the "carpetbaggers" whom they blamed for the whole situation. Reform and even Democratic tickets included Negro nominees. But the Negro people smelled a rat and understood that the leaders of the K.K.K. as well as the conciliators meant to deprive them of suffrage as soon as they gained power.

The reform Republican movements had the effect of drawing the native white elements out of the regular Republican Party. The Republican Party in the South became more and more a Negro Party which included a handful of white office-holders. In 1873 the *Montgomery Daily Advertiser*, the leading Democratic paper of Alabama, could triumphantly point out that Alabama had 98,000 colored citizens and 90,000 Republicans, Texas 51,575 Negroes and 51,846 Republicans, South Carolina 85,475 Negro citizens and 85,071 Republicans, Louisiana 86,913 Negro voters and about the same number of Republicans—"thus showing that the number of Republicans is regulated by the number of blacks in the states." [17]

In isolating the Negro people as the only mass support of the Radical Republican régimes, the bolters played into the hands of reaction. The struggle between revolution and counter-revolution in the South became largely a conflict between the Negro masses and the planters. When the North refused military and other aid and deserted the battlefield, it became only a question of time before the Negro people would be defeated by far superior forces.

The Counter-Revolutionary Coup d'États

REACTION, or "home rule"—as the historians are fond of terming it—triumphed in state after state, but not without a sharp struggle. In Texas extensive K.K.K. activity kept the Negroes from the polls in 1872. The Democrats won the legislature and elected all congressmen. The Radical Governor was ready to hold the capitol with the aid of the Negro militia. But the President refused to send military reënforcements and the Republicans were forced to withdraw. Again in 1874 the Republicans refused to recognize a Democratic victory, won by terror. Both sides armed themselves and seized various government buildings. But Washington, the final arbiter in these matters, supported the reactionaries.

A reign of K.K.K. terror, dignified with the title of "campaign for liberation," and marked by the murder of a number of Republican and Negro leaders, gave the Democrats in Alabama the governorship and a majority in the legislature in 1874. The Negroes in the Black Belt counties armed and reorganized their militia companies on the eve of the election and succeeded in sending 35 Negro Republicans to the reactionary legislature.

In Arkansas the split-off wing of the Republican Party became the instrument of reaction. As a result of the 1872 elections both the Radical and the Conservative Republicans claimed the governorship. Armed conflict between the contending factions broke out at Austin and Helena, where armed Negroes attempted to maintain their elected people in office.[18] Dual government existed in the state until 1874. Both sides had armed men and waged open battles in Little Rock. One side captured the State House and the other seized the telegraph station and the railroad. President Grant recognized the Conservatives and as a result the Democrats elected the legislature and the governor. Too late the President objected to the seizure of power by the reactionaries as a "violent revolution." Congress recognized the Bourbon government.

Most violent struggles occurred in Mississippi, Louisiana and South Carolina. In the two latter states reaction was installed only by the intervention of the North after the national elections of 1876.

The prelude to Bourbon victory in Mississippi was the split of the Republican Party in 1873. The Radical Republican Ames was elected Governor by the Negro vote against Senator Alcorn, former Governor, who ran on the Conservative Republican ticket and was supported by the Democrats. As in other states the split among the Republicans, signifying the rupture of the Negro-"scalawag" coalition, inaugurated the counter-revolutionary onslaught. One of the largest of the so-called riots occurred at Vicksburg in 1874, when a "committee of tax-payers" 500 strong marched on the town, forced the white Republican sheriff and Negro chancery clerk to resign, and installed their own people into office. Governor Ames called upon the captain of the Negro militia to suppress the usurpers. Negroes from the surrounding plantations marched on the town. A pitched battle was avoided when leaders of both sides agreed to withdraw, but as the Negro force proceeded to do so they were fired upon and a number were killed.[19] Other attacks by "tax-payers committees" on a smaller scale occurred throughout the state. Governor Ames wired the President informing him that unlawful infantry and cavalry organizations existed in Vicksburg and that they also had a few pieces of artillery. Grant's reply to the demand for Federal troops was typical: "The whole public are tired out with these autumnal outbreaks in the South, and the great majority are ready now to condemn any interference on the part of the Government."

The election campaign of 1875 was in reality civil war turned into massacre. The armed Bourbon leagues attacked political rallies of Negroes or at the point of guns made them listen to streams of abuse from Democratic orators. At Clinton, where 1,500 Negroes and about 100 whites were attending a Republican barbecue, Democrats fired into the crowd. Special trainloads of armed mobs came from the nearby cities to the aid of the instigators of the riot. At least 50 Negroes were killed on sight. When Grant refused to send troops, the legislature authorized the purchase of additional guns and ammunition and the Governor called for the mobilization of the militia in a manifesto, "To Arms!" The Democratic *Clarion* retorted: "The time has come when the companies that have been organized for protective and defensive purposes should come to the front... Let every citizen hold himself in readiness to join one of these companies." When conflict on a large scale seemed about to break out, the Governor gave in and signed a "Peace Agreement" with the Democrats. The Negro militias were disbanded and disarmed on the promise of the Democrats that they would permit Negroes to vote. The "Peace Agreement" sounded the death-knell of Radical Republican power in Mississippi.

What followed came to be known as the "Mississippi Plan for the restoration of home rule." It was nothing but outright terror and massacre of the now defenseless Negroes. On election day they were kept from the polls. In Yazoo, for example, the Republican vote in 1873 was 2,427 and in 1875 it was seven. The Democrats gained a large majority in the legislature, elected nearly all county officials and chose four out of six congressmen. President Grant characterized the new régime as follows: "Mississippi is governed today by officials chosen through fraud and violence such as would scarcely be accredited to savages, much less to civilized and Christian people." The Republican Governor and Lieutenant-Governor were forced to resign and leave the state. One of the first acts of the new legislature was to repeal the tax measures.

Typical of the ferocity of the counter-revolution was the fate of five Reconstruction leaders of the state who were active since the first "Black-and-Tan Convention." One was assassinated on the streets of Clinton; another was hanged by the Klan; one was shot in broad daylight and still another was shot in the courthouse at Yazoo City, while a fifth was found dead in a waterhole.[20] The Boutwell Committee, appointed by Congress, investigated the Mississippi elections. It had to admit that the Democratic victory was due to terror and outrages against the Negroes, that the legislature thus elected was not a legal body and that the state was "under the control of political organizations composed largely of armed men whose common purpose is to deprive the Negroes of the free exercise of the right of suffrage and to establish and maintain the supremacy of the white-line Democracy."[21] But Congress let reaction be.

Counter-revolution followed essentially the same pattern in Louisiana and South Carolina: first a split in the Republican Party, then a reign of White Terror, the existence of dual governments, and finally the establishment of counter-revolutionary power, this time with the direct aid of the North.

In Louisiana, the split-off Republicans fused with the Democrats in 1872, but the Radical Republicans were able to retain power with the aid of troops. White Terror took a heavy toll in the Colfax and Coushatta massacres in 1873. At Colfax on Easter Sunday the Bourbons attacked with cannon a Negro force entrenched in the courthouse. The courthouse was fired and 61 were killed as they fled; 37 Negroes were shot in cold blood after they had been taken prisoner. At Coushatta six Negroes were killed after they had surrendered. In New Orleans, civil war broke out between the White Leagues and the Negro police. Federal troops ousted the Bourbon forces from the State House. In the elections of 1874 both sides claimed victory and dual governments were preparing for war. General Sheridan, in command of the Federal troops, recognized the Republicans and earnestly urged Congress to take decisive action against the "banditti." The Chicago *Tribune* was at first inclined to demand Federal interference in behalf of the Republican régime but when it learned that "those leading the revolution were the leading men of New Orleans, and not the 'riff-raff' of the town," it was inclined to the view "that the best thing the National Government can do is to let well enough alone." [22] Northern Republicans evidently felt the same way about it for their committee sent to investigate finally established a compromise which gave the Democrats a majority in the Lower House.

In South Carolina the first split among the Republicans occurred in 1870, when the Union Reform Party gained the support of the Democrats. At the nominating convention of the Party in 1872, about one-third of the Republican delegates withdrew. The Radical Republicans retained their hold but the bolters won ten counties of which eight were in the up-country. In the 1874 elections the Radicals won again by a small margin over the bolters, who received Democratic support. But Chamberlain, the new Radical Governor, was extremely conciliatory under the pressure of the Right. He appointed a number of Conservatives as judges, disbanded the Negro militia in a county where it was most needed, alleviated taxes against the large planters and, in general, started the work which the counter-revolution finished in 1876.

The K.K.K. and similar organizations were extremely active in the state. Taxpayers' conventions were held and in 1874 tax unions were organized by the large property-holders throughout the state. The cry of reaction was: "Old men in the Tax Unions and

"The 'Bloody Shirt' Reformed: Governor Tilden, 'It is not I, but the Idea of Reform which I represent,'"—By Nast, *Harpers Weekly,* Aug. 12, 1876.

young men in the rifle clubs!" The "Mississippi Plan" was adopted in the election campaign of 1876 and a *coup d'état* was contemplated for election day. General Wade Hampton was nominated by the Democrats on an outright reactionary program to run against Chamberlain. The situation became so tense, and the Presidential campaign was so uncertain, that President Grant sent Federal troops. Both sides claimed victory and dual governments were established.

The results of the Presidential election of 1876 were close. Tilden, the Democratic candidate, had 184 electoral votes; he needed one more vote to be proclaimed President. Hayes, the Republican, had 166 undisputed votes; he claimed in addition South Carolina, Louisiana and Florida to give him the necessary 185 for election. If any one of these states was counted for Tilden he would win. In all three states, however, both sides claimed victory. The popular vote for Tilden was 4,300,000, for Hayes 4,036,000. Large numbers of Negroes, who would have cast their vote for the Republicans, had been intimidated away from the polls. The House of Representatives had a large Democratic majority and would give Tilden the election in the count of the electoral vote; the Senate was Republican and would give Hayes the election. The situation was tense. The country was again on the verge of civil war. Threats were heard of a Democrat-led march on Washington. Grant concentrated troops in and around the capital.[23]

After extended dickering, an electoral commission was finally established which gave Hayes the contested states of Florida, Louisiana, South Carolina and also Oregon, after a crisis which lasted three months. An agreement had been reached behind the scenes, while the electoral vote was being counted. Through intermediaries, Hayes assured the Southern Democrats that in return for the Presidency he would grant them complete control of South Carolina and Louisiana. The Republican Party bought its victory at the price of completely abandoning the Negro masses to the tender mercies of the counter-revolution. History is favored with a written record of the treachery. The document, dated February 27, 1877, drawn up by Stanley Matthews and Charles Foster of Ohio, close personal and political friends of Hayes, recorded the essence of conversations with Senator John B. Gordon of Georgia and Representative J. Young Brown of Kentucky:

Referring to the conversation had with you yesterday in which Governor Hayes' policy as to the status of certain Southern states was discussed, we desire to say that we can assure you in the strongest possible manner of our great desire to have him adopt such a policy as will give the people of the States of South Carolina and Louisiana the right to control their own affairs in their own way, subject only to the Constitution of the United States and the laws made in pursuance thereof, and to say further that from an acquaintance with and knowledge of Governor Hayes and his views, we have the most complete confidence that such will be the policy of his administration.[24]

There were probably additional private assurances as the electoral vote was counted. For as soon as it became evident that the Electoral Commission would favor Hayes, Benjamin H. Hill called together 42 ex-Confederate members of the House, who pledged themselves to support the count.[25]

Hayes fulfilled his obligations under the agreement to the letter. Dual governments existed in South Carolina and Louisiana. After a conference with General Hampton and Governor Chamberlain, Hayes withdrew the Federal troops from the state house at Columbia on April 10, 1877, and the government was turned over to the counter-revolutionary cohorts of Wade Hampton. On April 20, he ordered the troops withdrawn from the State House in New Orleans, and the reactionary régime was installed.[26] The Republicans were ousted from the Florida government in January 1877 by a decision of the State Supreme Court.

Counter-revolution in the South was triumphant. The bourgeoisie had bargained away the revolution in step after step until it placed its own seal of approval upon victorious reaction. It has kept its pledge, as given to the Bourbons of 1876, to the present day.

CHAPTER VIII

SUMMARY

In general outline the processes of Reconstruction were made inevitable by the Northern victory in the Civil War. Destruction of the slave system was the irrevocable outcome. The second phase of the revolution could develop only on the basis of this great accomplishment. Reconstruction was the continuation of the Civil War into a new phase, in which the revolution passed from the stage of armed conflict into primarily a political struggle which sought to consolidate the Northern triumph.

On a national scale, the basic problem of the period was solved by perpetuating the defeat of the former slavemasters long enough to permit the consolidation of bourgeois power. Thus, in the broad historical sense, Reconstruction achieved its purpose in preventing the return of chattel slavery and in placing the immediate future of the nation in the hands of the industrial monarchs. The war destroyed the chief obstacle to the growth of capitalism. Reconstruction established the conditions for the rapid evolution of large-scale manufacture and monopoly.

Capitalism, however, can proceed on the main course of its development in a number of ways. Within the general framework of its historic purposes, it may adopt freer and more democratic or less free and less democratic paths. During Reconstruction the revolutionary method was attempted. The Northern party sought to extend the gains of the Civil War, to establish popular democracy in the South, and this effort

produced one of the most glorious chapters in our revolutionary and democratic heritage. For in order to
establish democracy in the South it was necessary
above all to guarantee democracy for the freedmen,
which meant to reverse completely the social and political structure of the slave oligarchy. A fundamental
agrarian and democratic upsurge was released which
provided the principal revolutionary aspect of Reconstruction. All other problems of the period—and there
were many—have to be related to this historic democratic transformation which fell within the domain of
the bourgeois revolution, and which was possible of
achievement even within the framework of the new
phase of capitalist development.

Vital revolutionary weapons were employed in the
fight for democracy in the South. During the Civil
War the bourgeoisie had to adopt revolutionary methods—armed conflict against the counter-revolution,
emancipation of the slaves, and the arming of the
Negroes. During Reconstruction it also had to apply
revolutionary methods to maintain the hard-won victory—a bourgeois-democratic dictatorship over the
conquered slavemasters, the disfranchising of the old
rulers, and the conferring of the ballot and other civil
rights upon the freedmen as well as upon new sections
of the white population.

Military rule was established by the Reconstruction
Acts, but these Acts also provided for popular support
of the dictatorship. As in other profound social revolutions of the capitalist era, there resulted a democratic
dictatorship, supported by the classes placed in power
by the social overturn, which was entrusted with the
task of suppressing the counter-revolution while at the
same time it made possible the widest democracy yet
enjoyed by the masses. The upheaval was all the more
profound because slaves were overnight granted the

full rights of democracy within the bounds, of course, of the capitalist relationships. Rarely in history had an enslaved people so rapidly taken up the cudgels in a struggle for bourgeois democracy, fully and most intimately aware of the issues of the new epoch, a powerful force on the side of progress. The revolution forged new instruments—the Union Leagues, the citizen's militias, the people's assemblies—with which to destroy the old slavocrat state, and erect a new state edifice in the domain of the Confederacy. The broadest masses of the oppressed classes were encompassed in the democratic dictatorships which for a time ruled the Radically Reconstructed states.

The revolution was forced to recede from this high level, to surrender one advance position after another to the counter-revolution. The prime decision of the Civil War could not be reversed, but reaction was able to establish a Johnsonian South. Some of the democratic advances of Reconstruction still linger on. Democracy, however, was effectively crushed. By 1900-1902, every state had written "home-rule" into the new constitutions of "grandfather clause" fame, thus giving formal and legal expression to the reactionary victory which had been completed in 1877. Not until 1915 did the Supreme Court declare the most obnoxious clause of the new organic laws unconstitutional; it also killed Charles Sumner's Civil Rights Bill, forced the repeal of the last portions of the Enforcement Acts by 1894, and has found ways of overlooking the South's denial of democratic rights to Negroes. The Fourteenth and Fifteenth Amendments, the quintessence of the greatest victories of Reconstruction, remain promissory notes upon which the Negro people still have to collect. Such were the consequences of a whole series of fatal retreats which culminated in the peace agreement of

1876 and in the resulting victory of the *coup d'état* governments of the planters.

From the vantage point of our era of social change and of the problems which face us, it is possible to appreciate not only the grandeur and accomplishments but also the failures of Reconstruction. These failures are pregnant with vital lessons, for our country is still weighted by the issues which the revolutionary decade left unsolved. Of these issues the most vital was the land question. This problem was practically settled in favor of reaction during the Johnsonian relapse in the first years of Reconstruction. At the most favorable moment, when it would have altered the whole course of subsequent events, a basic revision of the land relationships in the South did not take place. This was the major cause for the defeat of democracy in the South. The large landed estates, which remained as the heritage of the slave system, were the soil on which half-free, half-slave labor developed. On the one hand, democracy for the freedmen was necessarily limited by their suppression in the economic sphere at a level where even partial exercise of political rights became increasingly difficult. On the other hand, the disfranchisement of a section of the ex-Confederate planters meant little as long as they retained the economic basis of political power.

Nor was it possible to alter the economic basis of political power in the South as long as the landed estates continued to hold the dominant position in the economic structure. The plantation hindered the free development of independent farm-holdings, of a diversified and rationalized agriculture, of an indigenous industry and, therefore, also delayed the growth of democratic classes. Democracy was deprived of its economic life-blood. This was the prime failure of Reconstruction, with the result that in the intervening years the remnants of the old slave system have grown into the present Southern system and recreate obstacles even today to the further economic and democratic development of the South. Counter-revolution found its natural support in the semi-feudal agrarian economy which emerged during Reconstruction.

Besides the partition of the estates, which would have solved the problem at one blow, there was still another progressive solution of the land question possible at that time. This was the course of agrarian reform which would gradually, but consistently, reduce the importance of the plantation in the general agriculture of the South. Steps in this direction were taken by the Reconstructed states when they increased taxation against the planters and passed legislation favoring small farmers. To some extent, landed estates were forced on the auction block and sold as small farmholdings, while a portion of the lands held by the government were offered for sale at low prices. A strong tendency to strike at the plantation system and to facilitate the growth of capitalist farmholdings as well as of free wage-labor was present in the activities of the Reconstruction governments. But, as a whole, the landed estates and the semi-feudal forms of labor remained. Consistent agrarian reforms could achieve their purpose only within a thoroughgoing democratic system in which popular government legislated directly against the planter and in favor of the farmers and middle classes. Because of the economic power of the planters, it was essential to utilize dictatorial measures to suppress the landlords politically while giving the freest reign to the democratic classes.

In this respect, the democratic dictatorship fell far short of its possibilities. As a class defeated in civil war and, for a time at least, deposed from power, the former slavemasters enjoyed unprecedented leniency.

Even during the Jacobin stage, amnesty was too readily extended to the ex-Confederate leaders. At no time were they restrained in their open agitational work against the Reconstructionists. Only on rare occasions were the most vicious Bourbon newspapers suppressed; generally they possessed the fullest freedom to fight freedom. The former slave oligarchy was permitted to engage in provocative appeals to "white superiority" and in dangerous agitation against "Negro Domination," until they succeeded in splitting the Radical Republican alliance. Inadequate and indecisive measures against them encouraged the armed bands of counter-revolution which terrorized the land and murdered thousands of Radical Republicans. Reaction was permitted to develop its armed counter-offensive, while the Northern party remained dangerously hesitant about arming the Negroes further and taking drastic measures against the threat to democracy.

So lenient was the bourgeoisie that even the President of the Confederacy was eventually released from prison and no person suffered the full consequences of defeat. The failure of the bourgeoisie to let loose the full measures of dictatorship against the class it had defeated in war gave this class a breathing spell in which to revive and regather its forces. If the bourgeoisie proved itself incapable of inaugurating a consistent offensive against the old ruling class, counter-revolution showed no hesitation about launching its own reign of terror against the people.

While the South was the main battlefield of Reconstruction, the whole nation was the stage for the vital inner conflict which characterized the period. The outcome of Reconstruction in the South was to a large measure determined by the regrouping of class forces in the country as a whole. In releasing the forces of industrial capitalism and in accelerating the settlement of the western farm lands, the Civil War produced profound changes throughout the country. As a result of the large land grants to the railroads, pioneers on the western plains were being expropriated, while farmers throughout the nation were robbed of their surpluses by excessive freight rates. Growing large-scale industry, with the aid of the high tariff and manipulations of financial promoters, charged high prices for industrial commodities while the farmers and the small urban producers were obtaining less for their products, suffering a sharp decline in real income. The handicraft and domestic industries were crumbling before the new industrial enterprises. Labor suffered from drastic declines in real wages. The growth of the industrial bourgeoisie set into motion whole strata of the population against the new leaders of the nation. New conditions were shifting the center of attack from the slave oligarchy to the industrial bourgeoisie.

Farmers and workers were first to revolt. By 1868, large sections of mid-Western farmers were already forming Granges and directing their attack against the financial oligarchy and the railroads. Trade unionism grew rapidly and labor was projecting its own political party. The non-industrial middle strata were alienated from Republican leadership by its services to the industrial and financial bourgeoisie. In their opposition to the "new oligarchy," however, the middle classes sought their ally on the Right. The Granges were throwing their support to the Democratic Party, particularly on the issue of money reform, while the platforms of that Party combined radical farm agitation with planks for general amnesty to the leaders of the counter-revolution and for a rapid restoration of the seceded states on a Johnsonian basis. Even the Labor Reform Party showed a dangerous affinity to the Democrats particularly on the question of money reform. In the South, the "poor whites" and the middle farmers were being won over by the Democrats principally on the issues of taxation, aid to the railroads and the "white superiority" program.

The middle classes were faced with an enigma. At no time can they provide a permanent base for political power. At most, the petty bourgeoisie can hold power only in a transitory phase, at a critical period of internal strife. The middle class may act as a balance of power for a time between two contending classes, allying itself with one or the other, but it must needs surrender its temporary political hold as soon as one or the other has been defeated. Such was the situation when Lincoln, the best spokesman of the middle classes, was President and controlled the policies of the nation. It did not take long for the industrial section of the bourgeoisie to seize national power when the slave oligarchy was downed. If the middle class strata were to play a political rôle they could do so only in the capacity of ally. And in the situation which arose after the Civil War they sought that ally in the defeated antagonist of the bourgeoisie. Johnson typified this course in the early stages of Reconstruction.

These contradictory currents within the bourgeois democracy caused the national split of 1872 in the Republican Party, the leader of the bourgeois revolution but at the same time the Party of the financial promoters and the industrialists. The Granger-Democratic coalition of the mid-West, the Reform Republican-Democratic combination of 1872, even the flirting of the young labor movement with the agrarian and Democratic money reformers contributed heavily to the victory of reaction in the South. The crisis of 1873 accelerated the gathering of all opposition forces. Faced with a formidable array of opponents in all parts of the country, the Republicans receded step by step from the advance positions gained during Reconstruction in an effort to allay the Bourbon counterattack. They finally ended by hitting off an agreement with the ex-Confederates, so that they could more easily face the opponents of the new era. In the presidential agreement of 1876, the Negroes were deserted in the most shameless manner, while the bourgeoisie at the same time succeeded in thwarting the middle class and labor opposition. The victory of counterrevolution in the South was therefore accompanied by the setting in of bourgeois reaction on a national scale, as exemplified by the violent suppression of the nation-wide railroad strike in 1877. On the basis of this new realignment of class forces, capitalism proceeded towards its stage of trusts and monopolies and unheard-of concentration of wealth.

Meanwhile, democracy had been doomed in the South. The issues of that revolutionary epoch of Reconstruction still persist—land, suffrage, civil rights—casting their shadow upon the whole country. They strike fire again, in a new setting and on a higher plane of social development. When the bourgeoisie betrayed democracy in the South it chalked up on the scoreboard of history a whole series of obligations which only the new revolutionary and progressive forces of our epoch can fulfill.

REFERENCE NOTES

INTRODUCTION

1. Karl Marx and Frederick Engels, *Correspondence, 1846-1895*, pp. 134-5.
2. Thomas F. Woodley, *Thaddeus Stevens*, pp. 366, 368, 379.
3. George E. McNeill, *The Labor Movement*, 1887, p. 122.
4. T. V. Powderly, *Thirty Years of Labor*, p. 57.
5. Engels, *Germany: Revolution and Counter-Revolution*, pp. 14-15.
6. Marx and Engels, *Gesamtausgabe (Collected Works), Dritte Abteilung* (Part Three), *Der Briefwechsel* (Correspondence), Berlin, 1931, Vol. 3, p. 109.

CHAPTER I

1. Francis B. Simkins and Robert H. Woody, *South Carolina During Reconstruction*, 1932, p. 15.
2. Frances B. Leigh, *Ten Years on a Georgia Plantation*, 1883, p. 132.
3. Woodley, p. 423.
4. Edward McPherson, *A Political Manual for 1866 and 1867 of Executive, Legislative, Judicial, Politico-Military and General Facts*, 1867, p. 141.

CHAPTER II

1. *Clarke County* (Ala.) *Journal*, June 11, 1863; quoted from *The Mississippian*.
2. J. G. de Roulhac Hamilton, *The Papers of Randolph Abbott Shotwell*, 1931, Vol. II, p. 253.
3. *The National Freedman*, monthly organ of the National Freedman's Relief Association, New York, April 1865.
4. A. A. Taylor, *Negro in Reconstruction of Virginia*, p. 35.
5. John R. Ficklen, *History of Reconstruction in Louisiana*, 1910, p. 136.
6. Walter L. Fleming, "Forty Acres and a Mule," *North American Review*, May 1906, p. 724.

7. General John Eaton, *Grant, Lincoln and the Freedmen*, 1907, p. 166.
8. Walter L. Fleming, *Documentary History of Reconstruction*, 1906, Vol. I, p. 75.
9. *Ibid.*, Vol. I, pp. 355-6; Sen. Doc. No. 27, 39th Cong., 1st Sess., p. 140.
10. *The National Freedman*, June 1865.
11. W. E. Burghardt Du Bois, *Black Reconstruction*, 1935, pp. 601-3.
12. *Weekly Advertiser,* Mobile, Ala., Sep. 9, 1865.
13. Sidney Andrews, "The South Since the War," in Fleming, *Documentary History*, Vol. I, pp. 357-8.
14. Whitelaw Reid, *After the War, A Southern Tour from May 1865 to May 1866.*
15. *Western Democrat*, Charlotte, N. C., Nov. 14, 1865.
16. Andrews, p. 36.
17. Fleming, *Documentary History*, Vol. I, pp. 353-4; Ho. Ex. Doc. No. 70, 39th Cong., 1st Sess.
18. *Clarke County Journal*, Sep. 21, 1865.
19. Jesse T. Wallace, *History of the Negroes in Mississippi*, 1927, p. 23.
20. Fleming, *Documentary History*, Vol. I, p. 90.
21. *Ibid.*, p. 83; Sen. Ex. Doc. No. 43, 39th Cong., 1st Sess.
22. McPherson, p. 68.
23. William W. Davis, *The Civil War and Reconstruction in Florida*, pp. 370-1.
24. James W. Garner, *Reconstruction in Mississippi*, 1901, p. 107.
25. Marx, *Briefwechsel*, Vol. IV, pp. 275-6.
26. *Ibid.*, Vol. 3, p. 110.
27. Letter to *The National Freedman*, July 1865.
28. Ho. Ex. Doc., 39th Cong., 2nd Sess., Vol. 3, No. 1, p. 740.
29. *Athens* (Ala.) *Post*, Feb. 3, 1866.
30. *Acts of Alabama*, 1865-66, p. 602.
31. Paul Lewinson, *Race, Class and Party*, p. 34.
32. Simkins and Woody, p. 229.
33. Fleming, "Forty Acres and a Mule," p. 727.
34. *The Liberator*, Dec. 29, 1865.
35. McPherson, p. 150.
36. *Savannah Republican*, quoted by Mobile *Daily Advertiser and Register*, Jan. 30, 1867.
37. *Clarke County Journal*, Dec. 7, 1865.
38. *Memphis Avalanche*, Oct. 9, 1866.
39. *Richmond Examiner*, quoted by Mobile *Daily Advertiser and Register*, March 7, 1867.
40. Quoted by *Western Democrat*, Jan. 26, 1869.
41. Fleming, "Forty Acres and a Mule," p. 732.

42. As occurred at a Republican mass meeting in Webster County, Georgia, in September 1868; *Moulton* (Ala.) *Advertiser*, Sep. 11, 1868.

43. Garner, p. 176.

44. Woodley, *op. cit.*, p. 481. Stevens' biographer cites as his authority the *Augusta* (Ga.) *Constitutionalist* (Sep. 7, 1867) and takes the matter for granted. But the whole thing might have been a piece of Bourbon propaganda to show Stevens' "dangerous" tendencies.

45. A letter quoted by George W. Julian, "Southern Land Grants," Speeches of Jan. 22 and 28, 1868, in the House of Representatives.

46. Thomas J. Woofter, *Negro Migration*, p. 38.

47. Leigh, p. 128.

48. See James S. Allen, *The Negro Question in the United States*, Chapters II and III for a description of the forms of labor as they developed in this period.

49. *Moulton Advertiser*, Sept. 18, 1868.

CHAPTER III

1. *The National Freedman*, August 1865.

2. Andrews, p. 125.

3. *The National Freedman*, Oct. 1865; McPherson, *op. cit.*, p. 18.

4. *Proceedings of Colored People's Convention of the State of South Carolina, Held in Zion Church, Charleston, November 1865*.

5. *The American Freedman*, published by the American Freedmen and Union Commission, Philadelphia, April 1866.

6. McPherson, pp. 52-3.

7. Fred A. Shannon, *Economic History of the People of the United States*, pp. 388-90.

8. Brookmire Economic Service, *Economic Trends of War and Reconstruction, 1860-1870*, pp. 18-27.

9. *13th Census of the United States*, 1910, Vol. VIII, "Manufactures," pp. 32-33.

10. Shannon, p. 436.

11. E. L. Bogart, *Economic History of the American People*, pp. 299-308.

12. Charles A. Beard and Mary R. Beard, *The Rise of American Civilization*, Vol. II, pp. 112-3. B. B. Kendrick, *The Journal of the Joint Committee on Reconstruction*, also makes it clear that the framers of the Fourteenth Amendment intended to protect corporate property against any restriction by the state governments.

13. Charles W. Collins, *Fourteenth Amendment and the States*, 1912, pp. 68 and 145.

14. George W. Julian, *Political Recollections, 1840-1872*, pp. 272-3.

CHAPTER IV

1. Woodrow Wilson, *History of the American People*. Vol. V, p. 22.
2. James F. Rhodes, *History of the United States*, Vol. VI, pp. 75, 76n.
3. Walter L. Fleming, *Documents Relating to Reconstruction*, No. 3, p. 3.
4. Davis, p. 375.
5. Fleming, *Documents*, No. 3, p. 4.
6. Edward A. Pollard, *Lost Cause Regained*, 1868, p. 143.
7. Fleming, *Documents*, No. 3, p. 5.
8. Simkins and Woody, p. 81.
9. A. T. Morgan, *Yazoo, or on the Picket Line of Freedom in the South, A Personal Narrative*, 1884, pp. 150-194.
10. James D. Lynch, *Kemper County Vindicated or a Peep at Radical Rule in Mississippi*, 1879, p. 234.
11. Simkins and Woody, pp. 82-3.
12. Garner, p. 180.
13. McPherson, pp. 253-4.
14. *Ibid.*, p. 250.
15. *Daily State Sentinel*, Montgomery, Ala., Jan. 16, 1868.
16. McPherson, p. 253.
17. Davis, pp. 485-6.
18. Simkins and Woody, p. 77.
19. Quoted by *Moulton Advertiser*, Sep. 18, 1868.
20. *Alabama Beacon*, Sep. 18, 1869.
21. *Athens Post*, Sep. 17, 1868.
22. *Alabama Beacon*, Nov. 6, 1868.
23. Taylor, p. 62.
24. Davis, p. 465.
25. *Weekly Advertiser*, Mobile, Jan. 27, 1868.
26. Fleming, *Documents*, Nos. 4-5.
27. Simkins and Woody, pp. 452-3.
28. *Daily State Sentinel*, Aug. 3, 1867.
29. *Ibid.*, May 21, 1867; *Athens Post*, May 16, 1867.
30. Rhodes, Vol. VI, p. 83.
31. See Allen, Chapters I and II.
32. See A. N. J. Den Hollander, "The Tradition of 'Poor Whites,'" in W. T. Couch, *Culture in the South*, 1934.
33. William E. Dodd, *The Cotton Kingdom*, 1921, p. 121.
34. Simkins and Woody, p. 41.
35. M. B. Hammond, *The Cotton Industry*, p. 127.

Chapter V

1. John W. Burgess, *Reconstruction and the Constitution*, 1902, p. 150.
2. Claude G. Bowers, *The Tragic Era*, p. 216.
3. Simkins and Woody, p. 91.
4. *Daily State Sentinel*, Nov. 16, 1867.
5. Garner, pp. 181, 187.
6. Fleming, *Documentary History*, Vol. I, p. 450.
7. Garner, pp. 193-5.
8. Simkins and Woody, p. 92.
9. *Proceedings of the Constitutional Convention of South Carolina*, 1868, pp. 115-18, 213.
10. *Independent Monitor*, Tuskaloosa, Ala., Feb. 19, 1868.
11. John R. Lynch, *Facts of Reconstruction*, 1913, pp. 92-4.
12. James S. Pike, *The Prostrate State, South Carolina Under Negro Government*, 1874, pp. 14-43.
13. Edward King, *The Great South*, 1875, p. 333.
14. *Ibid., passim.*
15. George Campbell, *White and Black, The Outcome of a Visit to the United States*, 1879, pp. 157-8; 177-8.
16. *Independent Monitor*, Aug. 11, 1868.
17. *Southern Argus*, Aug. 21, 1874.
18. Ficklen, p. 204.
19. *New York Tribune*, Oct. 23, 1868.
20. *Southern Argus*, May 8 and 29, 1874.
21. Shannon, p. 407.
22. *Fairfield Herald*, Nov. 20, 1872.

Chapter VI

1. *Selma Messenger*, March 17, 1866.
2. Montgomery *Daily Advertiser*, March 27, 1866.
3. Rhodes, Vol. V, pp. 203-4.
4. Shannon, p. 392.
5. Brookmire Economic Service, pp. 8-18.
6. James C. Sylvis, *The Life, Speeches, Labor and Essays of William H. Sylvis*, 1872, pp. 133-41.
7. McNeill, p. 128.
8. Karl Marx, *Capital*, International Publishers edition, Vol. I, p. 309.
9. Sylvis, p. 72.
10. *Ibid.*, pp. 77-82.
11. Hermann Schlüter, *Lincoln, Labor and Slavery*, pp. 231-34.
12. Richard Ely and others, *A Documentary History of American Industrial Society*, 1910, Vol. IX, pp. 157-60.
13. Quoted by *Workingman's Advocate*, Oct. 2, 1869.
14. Charles H. Wesley, *Negro Labor in the United States*, p. 165.

15. The proceedings of the congress are taken from the *Cincinnati Commercial* and the *Cincinnati Gazette*, both Republican, which printed the minutes, and from the *Workingman's Advocate*, supplemented by Commons and Associates, *History of Labor in the United States*, Vol. II; Wesley; and Richard Ely, *The Labor Movement in America*, 1886.
16. Sylvis, pp. 226-36.
17. *Ibid.*, pp. 331-48.
18. *Athens Post*, July 7, 1865.
19. *Athens Post*, Aug. 23, 1866.
20. Mobile *Daily Advertiser and Register*, April 2, 1867.
21. *National Workman*, Feb. 9, 1867.
22. *Workingman's Advocate*, Nov. 4, 1871.
23. Wesley, pp. 173-4; Commons, Vol. II, p. 137.
24. *Workingman's Advocate*, Nov. 6, 1869.
25. *Proceedings of the Colored National Labor Convention*, published by *The New Era*, Washington, 1870.
26. Ely, *Documentary History*, Vol. IX, pp. 243-53.
27. *Workingman's Advocate*, Jan. 1, 1870.
28. Wesley, p. 181.
29. Edward McPherson, *A Political History of the United States During Reconstruction*, p. 212.
30. Wesley, p. 188.
31. *Workingman's Advocate*, May 7 and April 9, 1870. Italics in original.
32. *New York Tribune* and *New York Sun*, Sep. 14, 1871.
33. *Workingman's Advocate*, April 13, 1872.
34. The account of the activities of the International Workingmen's Association is based on Hermann Schlüter, *Die Internationale in Amerika*, published in the *Sozialistische Arbeiter-Bibliothek* (Socialist Workers Library) by the German Section of the Socialist Party, Chicago, 1918.

Chapter VII

1. Quoted by Mobile *Daily Advertiser and Register*, April 16, 1867.
2. September 8, 1868.
3. *Moulton Advertiser*, Aug. 26, 1870.
4. Quoted by *Independent Monitor*, Nov. 6, 1867.
5. *Ibid.*, Feb. 5, 1868.
6. *Ibid.*, March 18, 1868.
7. *Daily State Sentinel*, Jan. 7, 1868.
8. Rhodes, Vol. VI, p. 318.
9. Albion W. Tourgee, *A Fool's Errand*, p. 226.
10. *The Nation*, April 10, 1872.
11. Simkins and Woody, pp. 277-8.
12. *State Documents*, 1869, pp. 10-15.

13. Quoted from the New York *Independent* by the *American Freedman*, Dec. 1866.
14. Simkins and Woody, p. 193.
15. Garner, p. 293.
16. *Daily State Sentinel*, July 12, 1867.
17. May 7, 1873.
18. Montgomery *Daily Advertiser*, Aug. 11-12, 1873.
19. Garner, pp. 333-4.
20. *Ibid.*, pp. 187-8; and Chap. XI.
21. McPherson, *A Political History*, p. 236.
22. Quoted by Montgomery *Daily Advertiser*, Sep. 16, 1874.
23. Rhodes, Vol. VII, pp. 245-6.
24. Charles R. Williams, *Life of Rutherford B. Hayes*, Vol. I, p. 533.
25. Rhodes, Vol. VII, p. 277.
26. Rhodes, Vol. VII, pp. 287-9.

APPENDICES

1

Special Field Orders No. 15

(William T. Sherman, *Memoirs*, Vol. II, p. 250 ff.)

Headquarters Military Division of the Mississippi
in the Field, Savannah, Georgia, January 16, 1865.

1. The islands from Charleston south, the abandoned
rice-fields along the rivers for thirty miles back from the
sea, and the country bordering the St. Johns River, Florida,
are reserved and set apart for the settlement of the Negroes
now made free by the acts of war and the proclamation of
the President of the United States.

2. At Beaufort, Hilton Head, Savannah, Fernandina, St.
Augustine and Jacksonville, the blacks may remain in their
chosen or accustomed vocations; but on the islands, and in
the settlements hereafter to be established, no white person
whatever, unless military officers and soldiers detailed for
duty, will be permitted to reside; and the sole and exclusive
management of affairs will be left to the freed peoples
themselves, subject only to the United States military authority, and the acts of Congress. By the laws of war, and
the orders of the President of the United States, the Negro
is free and must be dealt with as such. He cannot be subjected to conscription, or forced military service, save by
the written orders of the highest military authority of the
department, under such regulations as the President or
Congress may proscribe. Domestic servants, blacksmiths,
carpenters and other mechanics will be free to select their
own work and residence, but the young and able-bodied
Negroes must be encouraged to enlist as soldiers in the
service of the United States, to contribute their share
towards maintaining their own freedom and securing their
rights as citizens of the United States.

Negroes so enlisted will be organized into companies, battalions and regiments under the orders of the United States military authorities and will be paid, fed and clothed according to law. The bounties paid on enlistment may, with the consent of the recruit, go to assist his family and settlement in procuring agricultural implements, seed, tools, boots, clothing and other articles necessary for their livelihood.

3. Whenever three respectable Negroes, heads of families, shall desire to settle on land, and shall have selected for that purpose an island or locality clearly defined within the limits above designated, the Inspector of Settlements and Plantations will himself, by such subordinate officer as he may appoint, give them a license to settle such island or district, and afford them such assistance as he can to enable them to establish a peaceable agricultural settlement. The three parties named will subdivide the land under the supervision of the inspector, among themselves, and such others as may choose to settle near them, so that each family shall have a plot of not more than forty acres of tillable ground, and, when it borders on some water channel, with not more than eight hundred feet of water-front, in the possession of which land the military authorities will afford them protection until such time as they can protect themselves or until Congress shall regulate their title. The quartermaster may, on the requisition of the Inspector of Settlements and Plantations place at the disposal of the inspector one or more of the captured steamers to ply between the settlements and one or more of the commercial points heretofore named, in order to afford the settlers the opportunity to supply their necessary wants, and to sell the products of their land and labor.

4. Whenever a Negro has enlisted in the military service of the United States, he may locate his family in any one of the settlements at pleasure, and acquire a homestead, and all other rights and privileges of a settler, as though present in person. In like manner, Negroes may settle their families and engage on board the gunboats or in fishing, or in navigation of the islands waters, without losing any claim to land or other advantages derived from this system.

But no one, unless an actual settler as above defined, or unless absent on Government service, will be entitled to claim any right to land or property in any settlement by virtue of these orders.

5. In order to carry out this system of settlement, a general officer will be detailed as Inspector of Settlements and Plantations, whose duty it shall be to visit the settlements, to regulate their police and general arrangement, and who will furnish personally to each head of a family, subject to the approval of the President of the United States, a possessory title in writing, giving as near as possible the description of boundaries; and who shall adjust all claims or conflicts that may arise under the same, subject to the like approval, treating such titles altogether as possessory. The same general officer will also be charged with the enlistment and organization of the Negro recruits, and protecting their interests while absent from their settlements: and will be governed by the rules and regulations prescribed by the War Department for such purposes.

6. Brigadier-General R. Saxton is hereby appointed Inspector of Settlements and Plantations and will at once enter upon the performance of his duties. No change is intended or desired in the settlement now on Beaufort Island, nor will any rights to property heretofore acquired be affected thereby.

By order of Major-General W. T. Sherman
L. M. Dayton, Assistant Adjutant-General

Memorial to the Senate and House of Representatives of the United States in Congress Assembled

(*Proceedings of Colored People's Convention of South Carolina*)

Gentlemen:

We, the colored people of the State of South Carolina, in Convention assembled, respectfully present for your attention some prominent facts in relation to our present condition, and make a modest yet earnest appeal to your considerate judgment.

We, your memorialists, with profound gratitude to almighty God, recognize the great boon of freedom conferred upon us by the instrumentality of our late President, Abraham Lincoln, and the armies of the United States.

> *"The fixed decree, which not all Heaven can move,*
> *Thou, Fate, fulfill it; and, ye Powers, approve."*

We also recognize with liveliest gratitude the vast services of the Freedmen's Bureau together with the efforts of the good and wise throughout the land to raise up an oppressed and deeply injured people in the scale of civilized being, during the throbbings of a mighty revolution which must affect the future destiny of the world.

Conscious of the difficulties that surround our position, we would ask for no rights or privileges but such as rest upon the strong basis of justice and expediency, in view of the best interests of our entire country.

We ask first, that the strong arm of law and order be placed alike over the entire people of this State; that life and property be secured, and the laborer free to sell his labor as the merchant his goods.

We ask that a fair and impartial instruction be given to the pledges of the government to us concerning the land question.

We ask that the three great agents of civilized society—the school, the pulpit, the press—be as secure in South Carolina as in Massachusetts or Vermont.

We ask that equal suffrage be conferred upon us, in common with the white men of this State.

This we ask, because "all free governments derive their just powers from the consent of the governed"; and we are largely in the majority in this State, bearing for a long period the burden of onerous taxation, without a just representation. We ask for equal suffrage as a protection for the hostility evoked by our known faithfulness to our country and flag under all circumstances.

We ask that colored men shall not in every instance be tried by white men; and that neither by custom nor enactment shall we be excluded from the jury box.

We ask that, inasmuch as the Constitution of the United States explicitly declares that the right to keep and bear arms shall not be infringed and the Constitution is the Supreme law of the land—that the late efforts of the Legislature of this State to pass an act to deprive us of arms be forbidden, as a plain violation of the Constitution, and unjust to many of us in the highest degree, who have been soldiers, and purchased our muskets from the United States Government when mustered out of service.

We protest against any code of black laws the Legislature of this State may enact, and pray to be governed by the same laws that control other men. The right to assemble in peaceful convention, to discuss the political questions of the day; the right to enter upon all the avenues of agriculture, commerce, trade; to amass wealth by thrift and industry; the right to develop our whole being by all the appliances that belong to civilized society, cannot be questioned by any class of intelligent legislators.

We solemnly affirm and desire to live orderly and peacefully with all the people of this State; and commending this memorial to your considerate judgment.

Thus we ever pray.

Charleston, S. C., November 24, 1865
Zion Presbyterian Church.

3

Resolution of the Virginia Republican State Convention, April 17, 1867

(McPherson, *A Political Manual for 1866 and 1867*, pp. 253-4.)

Whereas—having for the first time in the history of Va. assembled at her State capital, at the call of a Union Republican State Committee, as a convention of Union men, for the purpose of ratifying the acts of the 39th and 40th Congresses, and adopting measures to unite all parties who earnestly and honestly desire that this legislation should be perfected in accordance with the express desire of Congress and carried out in good faith by the people of this State, we therefore in convention assembled, do

First, *Resolve*, that we return our sincere and heartfelt thanks to the 39th Congress for their recent legislation resulting in the passage of the Sherman-Shellabarger bill * and its supplement, and certify with gratitude that the beneficial effects of such legislation are already available in the increased security of loyal men, and in inducing immediate efforts towards reconstruction on the part of all classes; and that we do hereby pledge our earnest and persistent efforts to carry out in good faith, without evasion, with honesty of purpose, unflinching courage, and never-tiring energy, all its provisions believing that by this course alone can permanent peace and prosperity be restored to the state and an early admission to the Union be secured.

2. That in the principles of the National Republican Party of the United States we recognize all we can desire as a guide in our political future; that we adopt them as

---

* The Civil Rights Bill, passed by Congress over Johnson's veto on April 9, 1866, made Negroes citizens and provided punishment for persons who deprived them of civil rights under any state law. The Act was later replaced by the Fourteenth Amendment.

230

our platform, and pledge ourselves to their support, and cordially invite the cooperation of all classes of our fellow citizens, without distinction of race or color, without regard to former political opinions or action, induced by such convictions. We invite them to join us, and pledge them a warm welcome to our ranks, and a free and full participation in all the advantages of our organization. And firmly believing that in the present condition of public affairs the Republican Party offers the most available means through its organization for the speedy attainment of reconstruction, we do hereby adopt its principles and platform as the basis and platform of the Union Republican Party of Virginia.

3. That we adopt as part of our platform and as cardinal points in the policy of the Union Republican Party of Virginia the following propositions: first, equal protection to all men before the courts, and equal political rights in all respects including the right to hold office; second, a system of common-school education, which shall give to all classes free schools and a free and equal participation in all its benefits; third, a more just and equitable system of taxation, which shall apportion taxes to property, and require all to pay in proportion to their ability; fourth, a modification of the usury laws sufficient to induce foreign capital to seek investment in the State; fifth, encouragement to internal improvements and every possible inducement to immigration.

4. That in the noble utterances of the founders of our Constitution, we recognize a true appreciation of the great fact that parties or governments, to be prosperous or successful, must be founded or administered on the basis of exact and equal justice to all men; and we accept as our guides the great principles enunciated by them, first and most important of which is the great and glorious truth "that all men are created free and equal, are endowed with certain inalienable rights, and that among these are life, liberty and the pursuit of happiness," and we solemnly pledge on the part of this convention and the party it represents, a strict adhesion to these sentiments, which for the

first time in the history of Virginia, a political organization
is in a position to adopt in spirit and action as in name.

5. That believing the principles enunciated in the fore-
going resolutions can be objectionable to no man who really
loves the Union, and that they are the only true principles
which can give to Virginia an early restoration to the Union
and enduring peace and prosperity, we solemnly pledge
ourselves to support no man for an elective office who fails
to join us in their adoption and enforcement, who fails to
identify himself with the Union Republican Party in spirit
and action or hesitates to connect himself openly and
publicly with its platform as adopted here today.

6. That we recognize the great fact that interests of the
laboring classes of the State are identical, and that, without
regard to color, we desire to elevate them to their true position; that the exaltation of the poor and humble, the re-
straint of the rapacious and the arrogant, the lifting up
of the poor and degraded without humiliation or degradation to any; that the attainment of the greatest amount of
happiness and prosperity to the greatest number is our
warmest desire and shall have our earnest and persistent
efforts in their accomplishment; that while we desire to
see all men protected in full and equal proportions, and
every political right secured to the colored man that is enjoyed by any other class of citizens, we do not desire to
deprive the laboring white men of any rights or privileges
which they now enjoy, but do propose to extend those rights
and privileges by the organization of the Republican Party
in this State.

4

The First Reconstruction Act
March 2, 1867

(U. S. Statutes at Large, Vol. XIV, p. 428 ff.)

*An Act to provide for the more efficient Government
of the Rebel States*

Whereas no legal State governments or adequate protection for life or property now exists in the rebel States
of Virginia, North Carolina, South Carolina, Georgia, Mississippi, Alabama, Louisiana, Florida, Texas, and Arkansas;
and whereas it is necessary that peace and good order
should be enforced in said States until loyal and republican
state governments can be legally established: Therefore,

Be it enacted, That said rebel States shall be divided
into military districts and made subject to the military
authority of the United States as hereinafter prescribed,
and for that purpose Virginia shall constitute the first district; North Carolina and South Carolina the second district; Georgia, Alabama, and Florida the third district;
Mississippi and Arkansas the fourth district; and Louisiana
and Texas the fifth district.

Sec. 2. That it shall be the duty of the President to
assign to the command of each of said districts an officer of
the army, not below the rank of brigadier-general, and to
detail a sufficient military force to enable such officer to
perform his duties and enforce his authority within the
district to which he is assigned.

Sec. 3. That it shall be the duty of each officer assigned as aforesaid, to protect all persons in their rights of
persons and property, to suppress insurrection, disorder,
and violence and to punish, or cause to be punished, all
disturbers of the public peace and criminals; and to this
end he may allow local civil tribunals to take jurisdiction

233

of and to try offenders, or, when in his judgment it may be necessary for the trial of offenders, he shall have power to organize military commissions or tribunals for that purpose, and all interference under color of State authority with the exercise of military authority under this act, shall be null and void.

Sec. 4. That all persons put under military arrest by virtue of this act shall be tried without unnecessary delay, and no cruel or unusual punishment shall be inflicted, and no sentence of any military commission or tribunal hereby authorized, affecting the life or liberty of any person, shall be executed until it is approved by the officer in command of the district, and the laws and regulations for the government of the army shall not be affected by this act, except in so far as they conflict with its provisions: *Provided,* That no sentence of death under the provisions of this act shall be carried into effect without the approval of the President.

Sec. 5. That when the people of any one of said rebel States shall have formed a constitution of government in conformity with the Constitution of the United States in all respects, framed by a convention of delegates elected by the male citizens of said State, twenty-one years old and upward, of whatever race, color, or previous condition, who had been resident in said State for one year previous to the day of such election, except such as may be disfranchised for participation in the rebellion or for felony at common law, and when such constitution shall provide that the elective franchise shall be enjoyed by all such persons as have the qualifications herein stated for electors of delegates, and when such constitution shall be ratified by a majority of the persons voting on the question of ratification who are qualified as electors for delegates, and when such constitution shall have been submitted to Congress for examination and approval, and Congress shall have approved the same, and when said State, by a vote of its legislature elected under said constitution, shall have adopted the amendment to the Constitution of the United States, proposed by the Thirty-ninth Congress, and known as article fourteen, and when said article shall have become a part of the Constitution of the United States said State shall be declared entitled to representation in Congress, and senators and representatives shall be admitted therefrom on their taking the oath prescribed by law, and then and thereafter the preceding sections of this act shall be inoperative in said State: *Provided*, That no person excluded from the privilege of holding office by said proposed amendment to the Constitution of the United States, shall be eligible to election as a member of the convention to frame a constitution for any of said rebel States, nor shall any such person vote for members of such convention.

Sec. 6. That, until the people of said rebel States shall be by law admitted to representation in the Congress of the United States, any civil governments which may exist therein shall be deemed provisional only, and in all respects subject to the paramount authority of the United States at any time to abolish, modify, control, or supersede the same; and in all elections to any office under such provisional governments all persons shall be entitled to vote, and none others, who are entitled to vote, under the provisions of the fifth section of this act; and no persons shall be eligible to any office under any such provisional governments who would be disqualified from holding office under the provisions of the third *article* of said constitutional amendment.

5

Address of the Colored Convention to the People of Alabama

(*Daily State Sentinel,* May 21, 1867.)

Fellow Citizens: When, upon the passage of the Stevens [Sherman]-Shellabarger bill the colored people were invested with *all* the rights of manhood theretofore withheld from them, it was thought best that a convention, composed entirely of our own people, should be held, before deciding upon our future political course. Such a convention has been held in Mobile; it has deliberated upon the state of the country, upon the rights and duties of the colored people of Alabama, and authorized us, in its name, to issue this address to the voters of the State.

As there seems to be considerable difference of opinion concerning the "legal rights of the colored man," it will not be amiss to say that we claim exactly *the same rights, privileges and immunities as are enjoyed by white men*— we ask nothing more and will be content with nothing less. *All legal* distinctions between the races are now abolished. The word white is stricken from our laws, and every privilege which white men were formerly permitted to enjoy, merely because they were white men, now that word is stricken out, we are entitled to on the ground that we are men. *Color can no longer be pleaded for the purpose of curtailing privileges, and every public right, privilege and immunity is enjoyable by every individual member of the public.*—This is the touchstone that determines all these points. So long as a park or a street is a *public* park or street the entire public has the right to use it; so long as a car or a steamboat is a public conveyance, it must carry all who come to it, and serve all alike who pay alike. The law no longer knows white nor black, but simply men, and consequently we are entitled to ride in public conveyances, hold office, sit on juries and do everything else which we have in the past been prevented from doing solely on the ground of our color....

We have said that we intend to claim all our rights, and we submit to our white friends that it is the height of folly on their part to withhold them any longer. One-half of the voters in Alabama are black men, and in a few months there is to be an entire reorganization of the State government. The new officers—legislative, executive and judicial—will owe their election largely, if not mainly to the colored people, and every one must see clearly that the voters will then be certain to require and the officers to compel a cessation of all illegal discriminations. The question which every man now illegally discriminating against us has to decide is, whether it is politic to insist upon gratifying prejudices during a few dull months, with the certainty by so doing, of incurring the lasting displeasure of one-half of the voting population of the State. We can stand it if they can, but we assure them that they are being watched closely, and that their conduct will be remembered when we have power.

There are some good people who are always preaching patience and procrastination. They would have us wait a few months, years, or generations, until the whites voluntarily give us our rights, but we do not intend to wait one day longer than we are absolutely compelled to. Look at our demands, and then at theirs. We ask of them simply that they surrender unreasonable and unreasoning prejudice; that they cease imitating dog in the manger; that they consent to allow others as well as themselves to prosper and be happy. But they would have us pay for what we do not get; tramp through the broiling sun or pelting rain, or stand upon a platform, while empty seats mockingly invite us to rest our wearied limbs; our sick must suffer or submit to indignity; we must put up with inconvenience of every kind; and the virtuous aspirations of our children must be continually checked by the knowledge that no matter how upright their conduct, they will be looked on as less worthy of respect than the lowest wretch on earth who wears a white skin. We ask you—only while in public, however—to surrender your prejudices,—nothing but prejudices; and you ask us to sacrifice our personal comfort, health, pecuniary interests, self-respect, and the future prospects of our children. The men who make such requests must suppose us devoid of spirit and of brains, but they will find themselves mistaken. Solemnly and distinctly, we again say to you, men of Alabama, that we will not submit voluntarily to such infamous discrimination, and if you will insist upon tramping on the rights and outraging the feelings of those who are so soon to pass judgment upon you, then upon your own heads will rest the responsibility for the effect of your course.

All over the state of Alabama—all over the South indeed—the colored people have with singular unanimity, arrayed themselves under the Republican banner, upon the Republican platform, and it is confidently predicted that nine-tenths of them will vote the Republican ticket. Do you ask, why is this? we answer, because:

1. The Republican Party opposed and prohibited the extension of slavery.
2. It repealed the fugitive slave law.
3. It abolished slavery in the District of Columbia.
4. It abolished slavery in the rebellious states.
5. It abolished slavery throughout the rest of the Union.
6. It put down rebellion against the Union.
7. It passed the Freedmen's Bureau Bill and the Civil Rights Bill.
8. It enfranchised the colored people of the District of Columbia.
9. It enfranchised the colored people of the nine territories.
10. It enfranchised the colored people of the ten rebel states.
11. It provided for the formation of new constitutions and state governments in those ten states.
12. It passed new homestead laws, enabling the poor to obtain land.

In short, it has gone on, step by step, doing first one thing for us and then another, and it now proposes to enfranchise our people all over the Union. It is the only party which has ever attempted to extend our privileges, and as it has in the past always been trying to do this, it is but natural that we should trust it for the future.

While this has been the course of the Republican Party, the opposition has unitedly opposed every one of these measures, and it also now opposes the enfranchisement of our people in the North. Everywhere it has been against us in the past, and the great majority of its voters hate us as cordially now as ever before. It is sometimes alleged that the Republicans of the North have not been actuated by love for us in what they have done, and therefore that we should not join them; we answer that even if that were true they certainly never professed to hate us and the opposition party has always been denouncing the "d—n nigger and abolitionist" with equal fervor. When we had no votes to give, the opposition placed us and the Republicans in the same boat, and now we reckon we'll stay in it. It may be and probably is true that some men acting with the Republican Party have cared nothing for the principles of that party; but it is also certainly true that ninety-nine-hundredths of all those who were conscientiously in favor of our rights were and are in the Republican Party, and that the great mass of those who hated, slandered and abused us were and are in the opposition party.

The memories of the opposition must be short indeed, to have forgotten their language of the past twenty years but we have *not* forgotten it.

But, say some of the members of the opposition party, "We intend to turn over a new leaf, and will hereafter give you all your rights." Perhaps they would, but we prefer not to put the new wine of political equality into the old bottles of "sectional animosity" and "caste feeling." We are somewhat fearful that those who have always opposed the extensions of rights are not sincere in their professions. . . .

Another fact should be borne in mind. While a few conservatives are making guarded promises to us the masses of that party are cursing us, and doing all they can to "make the d—d niggers stay in their place." If we were, therefore, to join that party, it would be simply as servants, and not as equals. Some leaders, who needed our votes might treat us decently, but the great majority would expect us to stay at home until election day, and then vote as our employers dictated. This we respectfully decline doing. It seems to us safest to have as little as possible to do with those members of the community who delight to abuse us, and they are nearly, if not quite, all to be found in the ranks of the opposition party....

It cannot be disguised, however, that many men calling themselves conservatives are disposed to use unfair means to carry their points. The press of Mobile, and other parts of the State, contain numerous threats that those colored people who do not vote as their employers command, will be discharged; that the property-holders will combine, import white laborers, and discharge their colored hands, etc. Numerous instances have come to our knowledge of persons who have already been discharged because they attended Republican meetings, and great numbers more have been threatened. "Vote as we command, or starve," is the argument these men propose to make [use] of, and with it they expect to succeed.

In this expectation they will be mistaken, and we warn them before it is prosecuted any further, that their game is a dangerous one for themselves. The property which they hold was nearly all earned by the sweat of our brows—not theirs. It has been forfeited to the Government by the treason of its owners, and is liable to be confiscated whenever the Republican Party demands it. The great majority of that party is now opposed to confiscation, but if the owners of property use the power which it gives them to make political slaves of the poor, a cry will go up to Congress which will make the party a unit for confiscation.

Conservatives of Alabama, do you propose to rush upon certain destruction? Are you mad, that you threaten to pursue a policy which could only result in causing thousands of men to cry out to their leaders, "Our wives and little ones are starving because we stood by you; because we would not be slaves!" When the nation abolished slavery, you used your local governments to neutralize and defeat its action, and the nation answered by abolishing your governments and enfranchising us. If you now use your property to neutralize or defeat this, its last act, it will answer by taking away the property you are only allowed to retain through its unparalleled mercy and which you have proved yourselves so unworthy of retaining. . . .

So complete, indeed, will be our victory, that our opponents will become disheartened unless they can divide us. This is the great danger which we have to guard against. The most effectual method of preserving our unity will be for us to always act together—never to hold separate political meeting or caucuses. It may take some time for us to get to pulling together well, but perseverance and honest endeavor will overcome all obstacles. In nominations for office we expect that there will be no discriminations on account of color by either wing, but that the most capable and honest men will always be put in nomination. We understand full well that our people are too deficient in education to be generally qualified to fill the higher offices, but when qualified men are found, they must not be rejected for being black.

This lack of education, which is the consequence of our long servitude, and which so diminishes our powers for good, should not be allowed to characterize our children when they come upon the stage of action, and we therefore earnestly call upon every member of the Republican Party to demand the establishment of a thorough system of common schools throughout the state. It will benefit every citizen of the State, and, indeed, of the Union, for the well-being of each enures to the advantage of all. In a Republic, education is especially necessary, as the ignorant are always liable to be led astray by the arts of the demagogue.

With education secured to all; with the old and helpless properly cared for; with justice everywhere impartially administered, Alabama will commence a career of which she will have just cause to be proud. We shall all be prosperous and happy. The sad memories of the past will be forgotten amid the joys of the present and the prospect of the future.

And now, with our eyes fixed upon the starry emblem of our national greatness, and our hearts lifted in gratitude to God, we submit our cause to the good people of Alabama, and commend it to the favor of the Most High.

(Signed)   L. S. BERRY

WM. V. TURNER

R. D. WIGGINS

Committee

6

The Fourteenth Amendment

(Ratified July 28, 1868)

Art. XIV.

Sec. 1. All persons born or naturalized in the United States, and subject to the jurisdiction thereof, are citizens of the United States and of the State wherein they reside. No State shall make or enforce any law which shall abridge the privileges or immunities of citizens of the United States; nor shall any State deprive any person of life, liberty, or property, without due process of law; nor deny to any person within its jurisdiction the equal protection of the laws.

Sec. 2. Representatives shall be apportioned among the several States according to their respective numbers, counting the whole number of persons in each State, excluding Indians not taxed. But when the right to vote at any election for the choice of electors for President and Vice-President of the United States, Representatives in Congress, the Executive and Judicial officers of a State, or the members of the Legislature thereof, is denied to any of the male inhabitants of such State, being twenty-one years of age, and citizens of the United States, or in any way abridged, except for participation in rebellion, or other crime, the basis of representation therein shall be reduced in the proportion which the number of such male citizens shall bear to the whole number of male citizens twenty-one years of age in such State.

Sec. 3. No person shall be a Senator or Representative in Congress, or elector of President and Vice-President, or hold any office, civil or military, under the United States, or under any State, who, having previously taken an oath, as a member of Congress, or as an officer of the United

States, or as a member of any State legislature, or as an executive or judicial officer of any State, to support the Constitution of the United States, shall have engaged in insurrection or rebellion against the same, or given aid or comfort to the enemies thereof. But Congress may by a vote of two-thirds of each House, remove such disability.

Sec. 4. The validity of the public debt of the United States, authorized by law, including debts incurred for payment of pensions and bounties for services in suppressing insurrection or rebellion, shall not be questioned. But neither the United States nor any State shall assume or pay any debt or obligation incurred in aid of insurrection or rebellion against the United States, or any claim for the loss or emancipation of any slave; but all such debts, obligations and claims shall be held illegal and void.

Sec. 5. The Congress shall have power to enforce, by appropriate legislation, the provisions of this article.

7

The Fifteenth Amendment
(Ratified March 30, 1870)

Art. XV.

Sec. 1.   The right of citizens of the United States to vote shall not be denied or abridged by the United States, or by any State, on account of race, color, or previous condition of servitude.

Sec. 2.   The Congress shall have power to enforce this article by appropriate legislation.

8

(Schlüter, *Lincoln, Labor and Slavery*, pp. 230-32.)

Fellow Workmen:

In the inaugural address of our Association we said: "It was not the wisdom of the ruling classes, but the heroic resistance to their criminal folly by the working classes of England that saved the West of Europe from plunging headlong into an infamous crusade for the perpetuation and propagation of slavery on the other side of the Atlantic." It is now your turn to prevent a war whose direct result would be to throw back, for an indefinite period, the rising labor movement on both sides of the Atlantic.

We need hardly tell you that there are European powers anxiously engaged in fomenting a war between the United States and England. A glance at the statistics of commerce shows that the Russian export of raw products—and Russia has nothing else to export—was giving way to American competition when the Civil War tipped the scales. To turn the American ploughshare into a sword would at this time save from impending bankruptcy a power whom your republican statesmen in their wisdom had chosen for their confidential adviser. But disregarding the particular interests of this or that government, is it not in the general interest of our oppressors to disturb by a war the movement of rapidly extending international coöperation?

In our congratulatory address to Mr. Lincoln on the occasion of his reëlection to the Presidency * we expressed

---

* This was the first of three Addresses by the General Council of the International Workingmen's Association dealing directly with the Civil War. Written by Marx, it was approved November 29, 1864, two months after the formation of the Association. The

it as our conviction that the Civil War would prove to be as important to the progress of the working class as the War of Independence has been to the elevation of the middle class. And the successful close of the war against slavery has indeed inaugurated a new era in the annals of the working class. In the United States itself an independent labor movement has since arisen which the old parties and the professional politicians view with distrust. But to bear fruit it needs years of peace. To suppress it, a war between the United States and England would be the sure means.

The immediate tangible result of the Civil War was of course a deterioration of the condition of American workingmen. Both in the United States and in Europe the colossal burden of a public debt was shifted from hand to hand in order to settle it upon the shoulders of the working class. The prices of necessaries, remarks one of your statesmen, have risen 78 per cent since 1860, while the wages of simple manual labor have risen 50 and those of skilled labor 60 per cent. "Pauperism," he complains, "is increasing in America more rapidly than population." Moreover, the sufferings of the working class are in glaring contrast to the new-fangled luxury of financial aristocrats, shoddy aristocrats and other vermin bred by war. Still the Civil War offered a compensation in the liberation of the slaves and the impulse which it thereby gave to your own class movement. Another war, not sanctified by a sublime aim or a social necessity, but like the wars of the Old World, would forge chains for the free workingmen instead of sundering those of the slave. The accumulated misery which it would

Address to President Johnson (May 13, 1865), also written by Marx, transmitted the condolences of the General Council on the assassination of Lincoln and urged Johnson to continue boldly the work of reconstruction. A third Address, "To the People of the United States," September 25, 1865, congratulated them on the victory of the North and the abolition of slavery, and urged that full civil rights be accorded the Negro. (For the first two Addresses see K. Marx and F. Engels, *The Civil War in the United States*, 1937; these as well as the third Address are contained in Schlüter, *Lincoln, Labor and Slavery*.)

leave in its wake would furnish your capitalists at once with the motive and the means of separating the working class from their courageous and just aspirations by the soulless sword of a standing army. Yours, then, is the glorious task of seeing to it that at last the working class shall enter upon the scene of history, no longer as a servile following, but as an independent power, as a power imbued with a sense of its responsibility and capable of commanding peace where their would-be masters cry war.

INTERNATIONAL WORKINGMEN'S ASSOCIATION
London, May 12, 1869.

SELECTED BIBLIOGRAPHY

[The selected bibliography is intended for the reader who wishes to pursue the subject further. This list includes a number of books not cited by the author in the present volume.]

DOCUMENTARY SOURCES

H. S. COMMAGER, *Documents of American History*, vol. ii.

RICHARD ELY and Associates, *A Documentary History of American Industrial Society*, vols. ix and x (1860-1880).

WALTER L. FLEMING, *Documentary History of Reconstruction*, 2 vols.

BENJAMIN B. KENDRICK, *The Journal of the Joint Committee of Fifteen on Reconstruction* (39th Congress, 1865-67).

Ku Klux Conspiracy, The Testimony taken by the Joint Select Committee to inquire into the condition of affairs in the late insurrectionary states, 13 vols.

EDWARD McPHERSON, *A Political Manual for 1866 and 1867 of Executive, Legislative, Judicial, Politico-Military and General Facts.*

—— *A Political History of the United States During Reconstruction.*

Report of Senate Committee to Inquire into the Mississippi Elections of 1875, 2 vols., 44th Cong., 1st Sess., vol. 3, part 1.

CARL SCHURZ, *Report on Conditions of States of South Carolina, Georgia, etc.*, House Ex. Doc. No. 2, 39th Cong., 1st Sess.

U. S. Refugees, Freedmen and Abandoned Lands Bureau, *Annual Reports, 1865-1869.*

Contemporary Memoirs and Accounts

ELIZABETH H. BOTUME, *First Days Among the Contrabands.*

GEORGE CAMPBELL, *White and Black, the Outcome of a Visit to the United States.*

JOHN EATON, *Grant, Lincoln and the Freedmen.*

NORWOOD P. HALLOWELL, *The Negro as a Soldier in the War of the Rebellion.*

THOMAS W. HIGGINSON, *Army Life in a Black Regiment.*

EDWARD KING, *The Great South.*

HENRY LATHAM, *Black and White,* London.

FRANCES B. LEIGH, *Ten Years on a Georgia Plantation.*

JAMES D. LYNCH, *Kemper County Vindicated or a Peep at Radical Rule in Mississippi.*

JOHN R. LYNCH, *Facts of Reconstruction.*

—— *Some Historical Errors of James Ford Rhodes.*

GEORGE E. MCNEILL, *The Labor Movement.*

A. T. MORGAN, *Yazoo, or on the Picket Line of Freedom in the South.*

C. NORDHOFF, *Cotton States in the Spring and Summer of 1875.*

GEORGE W. NICHOLS, *The Story of the Great March.*

EDWARD L. PIERCE, "The Freedmen at Port Royal," *Atlantic Monthly,* vol. xii.

T. V. POWDERLY, *Thirty Years of Labor, 1859-1889.*

JAMES S. PIKE, *The Prostrate State, South Carolina Under Negro Government.*

WHITELAW REID, *After the War, A Southern Tour from May 1865 to May 1866.*

CHARLES STEARNS, *The Black Man of the South and the Rebels.*

JAMES C. SYLVIS, *The Life, Speeches, Labors and Essays of William H. Sylvis.*

ALBION W. TOURGEE, *A Fool's Errand.*

JOHN WALLACE, *Carpetbag Rule in Florida.*

H. C. WARMOUTH, *War, Politics and Reconstruction.*

Histories

HOWARD K. BEALE, *The Critical Year: A Study of Andrew Johnson and Reconstruction.*

CHARLES A. BEARD and MARY R. BEARD, *The Rise of American Civilization.*

JOHN W. BURGESS, *Reconstruction and the Constitution.*

GEORGES CLEMENCEAU, *History of American Reconstruction.*

JOHN R. COMMONS and Associates, *History of Labor in the United States.*

E. M. COULTER, *Civil War and Reconstruction in Kentucky.*

WILLIAM W. DAVIS, *The Civil War and Reconstruction in Florida.*

W. E. BURGHARDT DU BOIS, *Black Reconstruction.*

W. A. DUNNING, *Essays on Civil War and Reconstruction.*

—— *Reconstruction, Political and Economic.*

H. J. ECKENRODE, *Political History of Virginia during Reconstruction.*

WALTER L. FLEMING, *Freedmen's Savings Bank.*

—— *Civil War and Reconstruction in Alabama.*

—— *Sequel to Appomattox.*

—— *"Forty Acres and a Mule," North American Review,* May, 1906.

JOHN R. FICKLEN, *History of Reconstruction in Louisiana.*

JAMES W. GARNER, *Reconstruction in Mississippi.*

J. G. DE R. HAMILTON, *Reconstruction in North Carolina.*

ELLA LONN, *Reconstruction in Louisiana after 1868.*

GEORGE F. MILTON, *The Age of Hate.*

ALLAN NEVINS, *Emergence of Modern America, 1865-1878.*

ELLIS P. OBERHOLTZER, *History of the United States Since the Civil War,* vols. i, ii, iii.

PAUL S. PIERCE, *The Freedmen's Bureau.*

JAMES W. PATTON, *The Reconstruction of Tennessee.*

C. W. RAMSDELL, *Reconstruction in Texas.*

J. G. RANDALL, *The Civil War and Reconstruction.*

JAMES F. RHODES, *History of the United States Since the Compromise of 1850,* vols. vi, vii.

HERMANN SCHLÜTER, *Lincoln, Labor and Slavery.*

—— *Die Internationale in Amerika.*

FRANCIS B. SIMKINS and ROBERT H. WOODY, *South Carolina during Reconstruction.*

FRED A. SHANNON, *Economic History of the People of the United States.*

A. A. Taylor, *Negro in the Reconstruction of Virginia.*
—— *The Negro in South Carolina during Reconstruction.*
C. M. Thompson, *Reconstruction in Georgia.*
Jesse T. Wallace, *History of the Negroes in Mississippi.*
Laura Webster, *Operation of the Freedmen's Bureau in South Carolina.*
Charles H. Wesley, *Negro Labor in the United States.*
E. C. Wooley, *Reconstruction of Georgia.*

James S. Allen, *The Negro Question in the United States.*
Robert P. Brooks, *The Agrarian Revolution in Georgia, 1865-1912.*
William E. Dodd, *The Cotton Kingdom.*
Paul Lewinson, *Race, Class and Party: A History of Negro Suffrage and White Politics in the South.*
Karl Marx and Frederick Engels, *The Civil War in the United States* (1937).
—— *Correspondence, 1846-1895.*
"Some Negro Members of Reconstruction Conventions and Legislatures and of Congress," *Journal of Negro History,* vol. v, nos. 1 and 2.
Thomas F. Woodley, *Thaddeus Stevens.*

INDEX

Abolition movement, 24, 135, 176.
Adams, C. F., 191.
Alabama, Colored Convention of 1867, 103; registration of voters, 106; Constitutional Convention of 1868, 117; Constitution of 1868, 118, 122 *ff.*; readmitted, 126; reaction, 198.
Alcorn, J. L., 199.
Amendment, Thirteenth, 39, 42, 77; Fourteenth, 83 *ff.*, 86, 88, 118, 126, 137, 139, 209, 243, 244; Fifteenth, 137, 187, 209, 245.
Ames, Governor A., 199.
Amnesty, of former Confederates, 189, 212, 213; Johnson's proclamation of, 41; Lincoln's proclamation of, 36.
Amnesty Act of 1872, 189, 190.
Andrews, Sidney, 52, 53, 74.
Apportionment, 37, 38, 85.
Arkansas, Presidential Reconstruction, 38; registration of voters, 106; Constitution of 1868, 118; readmitted, 126; Negroes in local government, 135; reaction, 198.
Astor, William, 80.

Banks, General, 47.
Belknap, W. W., 143 *n.*
Bingham, J. A., 83, 84.
Black Belt, 107.
"Black Cavalry," 66.
Black Codes, 51, 57 *ff.*, 75, 137.
Black Reconstruction, 91.
Boston Workingmen's Assembly, 159.
Bourgeoisie, Industrial, 79 *ff.*
Boutwell Committee, 201.
Bowers, C. G., 91, 116, 118.
Bradley, A. A., 159, 178.
Brown, J. E., 113.
Brown, J. Y., 205.
Brown, John, uprising, 179.
Burgess, J. W., 86, 91, 116.
Butler, B. F., 47.

Cain, R. H., 76, 120, 195.
Campbell, Sir George, 136.
Capital, 149.
Cardozo, F. L., 76, 120.
Carpetbaggers, 94, 96, 117, 181 *ff.*
Cary, S. F., 163.
Caulkers' and Ship Carpenters' Union, 146.

Chamberlain, D. H., 202, 204, 205.
Chase, S. P., 93.
Civil Rights Bill, of 1866, 83, 104; Charles Sumner's, 189, 209.
Clinton massacre, 199.
Colfax massacre, 201.
Colfax, Schuyler, 143 *n.*
Colored Caulkers' Trade Union of Baltimore, 157.
Colored National Labor Union, 159, 160, 165 *ff.*; first convention, 168; platform, 170, 171, 173; Prospectus of Bureau of Labor, 171; and Republican Party, 159 *ff.*, 169, 172, 173; second convention, 173; Southern States' Convention, 173.
Communards, Paris, 178.
Communist Club of New York, 175 *ff.*
Confederate Congress, 33.
Confederates, disfranchised, 31, 89, 106, 118, 210.
Confiscation Act of 1862, 46.
Confiscation of landed estates, 31, 33, 44, 45, 69, 97, 121; and Northern troops, 66; Stevens' proposal for, 69, 70; and taxes, 141.
Conkling, Roscoe, 84.
Constitutional Conventions of 1865, 57; of 1868, 59, 94, 112, 113, 116 *ff.*
Constitutions of 1868, 118 *ff.*, 137; fight for, 122 *ff.*
Cooke, Jay, 93.
Corruption as a political weapon, 140, 143, 144, 193, 195.
Cotton exchanges, 194.
Coushatta massacre, 201.
Credit Mobilier, 143.
Cummings, S. P., 159, 160, 162, 172.

Davis, Jefferson, 48, 134.
Delaney, M. R., 76.
DeLarge, R. C., 76.
Democratic Party, and labor, 160, 161, 169; and Mid-west farmers, 163, 186, 213; and Negro nominees, 182, 196; War Democrats, 39, 40.
Downing, G. T., 77, 169.
Douai, Adolph, 176.
Douglass, Frederick, 31, 77, 173, 174, 179.

253